THE LOOK OF ARCHITECTURE

Each year the **New York Public Library** and **Oxford University Press** invite a prominent figure in the arts and letters to give a series of lectures on a topic of his or her choice. The lectures become the basis of a book jointly published by the Library and the Press. The previous books in the series are *The Old World's New World* by C. Vann Woodward; *Culture of Complaint: The Fraying of America* by Robert Hughes; *Witches and Jesuits: Shakespeare's Macbeth* by Garry Wills; *Visions of the Future: The Distant Past, Yesterday, Today, Tomorrow* by Robert Heilbroner; *Doing Documentary Work* by Robert Coles; and *The Sun, the Genome, and the Internet* by Freeman J. Dyson.

OTHER BOOKS BY WITOLD RYBCZYNSKI

One Good Turn: A Natural History of the Screwdriver and the Screw

A Clearing in the Distance: Frederick Law Olmsted and America in the Nineteenth Century

A Place for Art: The Architecture of the National Gallery of Canada

City Life: Urban Expectations in a New World

Looking Around: A Journey Through Architecture

Waiting for the Weekend

The Most Beautiful House in the World

Home: A Short History of an Idea

Taming the Tiger: The Struggle to Control Technology

Paper Heroes: Appropriate Technology, Panacea or Pipe-dream?

THE LOOK OF ARCHITECTURE

Witold Rybczynski

THE NEW YORK PUBLIC LIBRARY

OXFORD
UNIVERSITY PRESS

OXFORD
UNIVERSITY PRESS

Oxford New York
Auckland Bangkok Buenos Aires Cape Town Chennai
Dar es Salaam Delhi Florence Hong Kong Istanbul Karachi Kolkata
Kuala Lumpur Madrid Melbourne Mexico City Mumbai
Nairobi São Paulo Shanghai Singapore Taipei Tokyo Toronto

and an associated company in Berlin

Published by Oxford University Press, Inc.
198 Madison Avenue, New York, New York 10016

www.oup.com

Library of Congress Cataloging-in-Publication Data is available
ISBN 0-19-513443-5 (cloth) ISBN 0-19-515633-1 (pbk)

PHOTO CREDITS

Fig. 1. Courtesy of the University of Pennsylvania Archives. Fig. 2. Courtesy of the University of Pennsylvania Archives. Fig. 3. Bridgeman Art Library International. Fig. 4. Art Resource. Fig. 5. Toledo Museum of Art. Fig. 6. Foto Marburg/Art Resource. Fig. 7. Photo ©Albert Pfeiffer. Fig. 8. Photo by Morley Baer. Copyright of the Morley Baer Foundation. Fig. 9. Copyright unknown. Fig. 10. GreatBuildings.com. Photo © Donald Corner and Jenny Young. Fig. 11. Courtesy of the Library of Congress. Fig. 12. Detail. Courtesy of the Museum of the City of New York. Fig. 13. © Empire State Building Company. Fig. 14. Courtesy of the Library of Congress. Fig. 15. Courtesy of the Museum of the City of New York. Fig. 16. Courtesy of Radio City Music Hall. Fig. 17. Courtesy of the Lewis Walpole Library, Yale University. Fig. 18. ©PictureQuest/Photodisc. Fig. 19. ©TimePix. Fig. 20. Courtesy of the University of Pennsylvania Archives. Fig. 21. Courtesy of the Museum of the City of New York. Fig. 22. ©Jose Fuste Raga/eStock Photography/PictureQuest. Fig. 23. ©Judith Turner. Fig. 25. Fig. 24. ©Robert Lautmann. Courtesy of the author. Fig. 26. photo © Rollin La France. Courtesy of Venturi, Scott Brown and Associates. Fig. 27 and 28. Courtesy of the Allan Greenberg Associates. Figs. 29 and 30. © Robert Lautman. Fig. 31 and 32. Courtesy of TEN Arquitectos. Fig. 33. Used with permission of the Biltmore Estate, Asheville, North Carolina. Fig. 34. ©Jose Fuste Raga/eStock Photography/PictureQuest.

1 3 5 7 9 8 6 4 2
Printed in the United States of America
on acid-free paper

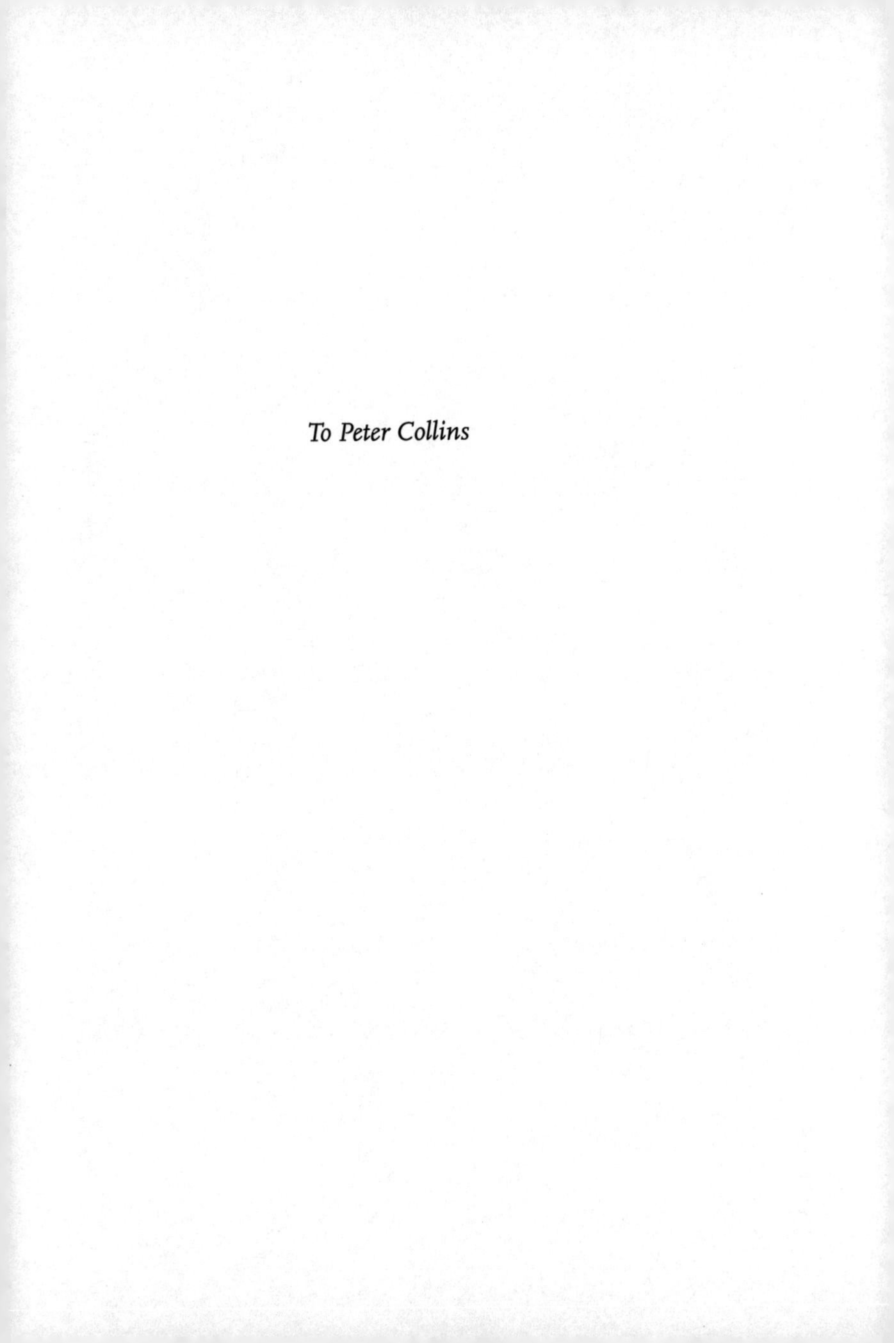

To Peter Collins

Contents

Introduction

Architects don't like to talk about style. Ask an architect what style he works in and you are likely to be met with a pained expression, or with silence. Press further, and you will provoke an exasperated denial: "Serious architecture has nothing to do with style." While a writer or a painter can be applauded for stylistic ability, calling an architect a stylist is considered faint praise. And nothing enrages an architect as much as being categorized according to a particular style. I have heard both Robert Venturi and Michael Graves bridle at the suggestion that their work had something to do with Postmodernism—of which both men are virtuoso practitioners. Most architects prefer to talk about massing and space, or context and historical allusions, or—if they are prone to academic jargon—about "tectonics" and "materiality." In other words, although architects are willing to accept the notion that buildings embody ideas, they don't like to acknowledge the manner in which these ideas are expressed.

Even a cursory glance at buildings of the recent past confirms that architectural style is real, and that, like style in dress or food, it changes with regularity. Different periods favor different materials: For example, glass-blocks belong to the 1920s, and corrugated fiberglass marks the 1950s; we will likely remember the late 1990s as the time that architects began wrapping buildings in zinc and titanium. The same is true for shapes and colors. There is no mistaking a cumbrous, monochrome prewar post office building, say, with its flimsy, pastel-colored Postmodern successor—the buildings, like stamps, have different styles.

One of the few modern architects early to face the issue of style was the iconoclastic Philip Johnson. "A style is not a set of rules or shackles, as some of my colleagues seem to think," he once said. "A style is a climate in which to operate, a springboard to leap further into the air." In 1932, Johnson and Henry-Russell Hitchcock pointedly described the new architecture of flat-roofs, white rectilinear façades, and ship-railing balconies as the International *Style*. At the time, Johnson was an architectural historian; practitioners themselves bridled at being associated with something so trivial. "Style is like a feather in a woman's hat, nothing more," sniffed Le Corbusier. Gabrielle Chanel, who knew something about women's hats, saw things differently. "Fashion passes," she said, "style remains."

I agree with Chanel. It seems to me that style is one of the enduring—and endearing—aspects of architecture. Architects are being naïve in denying validity to the concept of style. They are also being dishonest, since most successful practitioners are acutely conscious of style—and not only in their designs. How else to characterize Frank Lloyd Wright's capes and pork-pie hats, Le Corbusier's round eyeglasses, and Louis Kahn's bow ties, except as evocations of personal style? Even Frank Gehry's rumpled suits are a kind of style. In fact, most of the architects I know are preoccupied with style—not only in dress, but in furniture, automobiles, even pens (the cigarlike Mont Blanc Meisterstück being the favorite). Why are they unwilling to acknowledge the obvious?

I have explored tentatively the subjects of style in essays and book reviews over the years. My first public lecture on dress and décor was at the 1994 International Design Conference at Aspen, later repeated at Colonial Williamsburg. I was given the opportunity to bring this material together in a considered manner when I was invited to give a series of public lectures under the auspices of Oxford University Press and the New York Public Library. I delivered the lectures in the Celeste Bartos Forum of the Library on three successive Tuesday evenings in October 1999. This book is the result. It is organized in three parts, which reflects the course of the lectures. However, the spoken and written word differ. This book is not a transcription of what was, in any case, an extemporaneous series of talks. I have taken the opportunity to elaborate ideas, which I previously merely alluded to. Reflection and some pointed questions from an attentive audience have caused me to reconsider certain statements. The text has been enriched further by conversations with practitioners, notably Jaquelin T. Robertson and Robert A. M. Stern. It was the latter who reminded me that Oscar Wilde once remarked, "In matters of importance, style is everything."

THE LOOK OF ARCHITECTURE

ONE
DRESSING UP

Architecture is hard to define. Goethe called it music frozen in space, which, while it captures a sense of rhythm, is too one-dimensional. And it relegates the mother of the arts to an inferior position; just as well to describe music as melted architecture. Nietzsche believed that architecture reflected his pride, man's triumph over gravity, and his will to power. This notion applies to many buildings, from Gothic cathedrals to skyscrapers, but it is too, well, Nietzschean. The British master Edwin Lutyens referred to architecture as a sort of play: "In architecture, Palladio is the game!" Le Corbusier described his art as "the masterly, correct and magnificent play of masses brought together in light," which is a good description of one of his own buildings. I am partial to Sir Henry Wotton's definition. Wotton, who lived a long time in Venice and was a lover of architecture though not an architect, published a treatise on the subject in 1642. "In Architecture, as in all other Operative Arts, the end must direct the Operation," he wrote. "The end is to build well. Well-building hath three conditions: Commoditie, Firmeness, and Delight."

Sir Henry's description, which was based on the writings of the Roman architect Vitruvius, appeals to me because it emphasizes the complexity of the building art. To begin with, architecture has not one but three distinct purposes: to shelter human activity (commodity), to durably challenge gravity and the elements (firmness), and to be an object of beauty (delight). Architecture is always a synthesis of the three. However, the fulfillment of one purpose does not guarantee the satisfaction of the others. There are homely sturdy buildings and beautiful flimsy ones. A well-planned building can be ugly just as a beautiful building can function poorly. Form does not, contrary to Louis Sullivan's hoary maxim, follow function.

Not only are function and form separate, over their long lives buildings can successfully accommodate a variety of uses. For example, some of the most famous museums (the Louvre, the Hermitage, the Belvedere) started life as royal palaces; the Uffizi in Florence is so named because it originally housed offices; and the Prado in Madrid was designed to be a museum of science, not art. The acclaimed Musée d'Orsay in Paris is housed in a railroad station. Two of my favorite small museums, the Frick Collection in New York City and the Phillips Collection in Washington, D.C., were built as residences. As historic preservation and adaptive reuse demonstrate, you can shop in a renovated warehouse, do office work in a converted loft, or live in a barn. Assuming, of course, that the warehouse, the loft, and the barn were well built. The material fabric of old buildings—the heavy beams, rough brick walls, and solid woodwork—is one of their chief pleasures. That is why we feel cheated by hollow walls, flimsy doors, and shaky balustrades. Buildings should last and feel as though they will.

One might assume that just as the highest-rated cars—Mercedes-Benz, BMW, Lexus—represent the highest standards of automobile technology, the most admired architecture would be the best built. This was generally true in the past, but in the twentieth century, when new materials and new aesthetic theories often have driven architects to cavalier experimentation, even celebrated architects have fallen short in that department. Le Corbusier's white suburban villas, for example, were crudely finished in cement plaster on top of brick, and since the architect usually ignored (for aesthetic reasons) intrusive metal flashing and coping strips, the crude "machines for living" often aged poorly. Some Frank Lloyd Wright buildings have leaky skylights, sagging overhangs, and defective heating systems. This does not make them any less delightful to visit, but it must make them considerably less delightful to inhabit. Perhaps the most dramatic example of failed experimentation in recent years is the Centre Georges Pompidou in Paris, which opened in 1977. The building was widely praised for its architectural innovation—the British periodical *Architectural Design* called it "a seminal building of the Modern Movement." The architects Renzo Piano and Richard Rogers turned the building literally inside-out. They dramatically hung pipes, ducts, fire stairs, elevators, and escalators from the exterior structure. These previously hidden elements were now exposed in plain sight—and exposed to the elements. The result might have been foreseen: after only twenty years, the French government was obliged to close the building for a two-year renovation. Although the authorities maintained that the renovation was required because of the unexpectedly large number of visitors, according to *Le Monde* almost half of the $90 million budget was spent on refurbishing the façade.

The University of Pennsylvania, where I teach, is the site of Louis I. Kahn's A. N. Richards Medical Research Laboratory. This structural tour-de-force of precast concrete and brick brought its designer international acclaim. I remember traveling from Montreal to Philadelphia as a student to

Fig. 1. A view of the "servant" and "served" spaces at Louis I. Kahn's A.N. Richards Laboratory at the University of Pennsylvania.

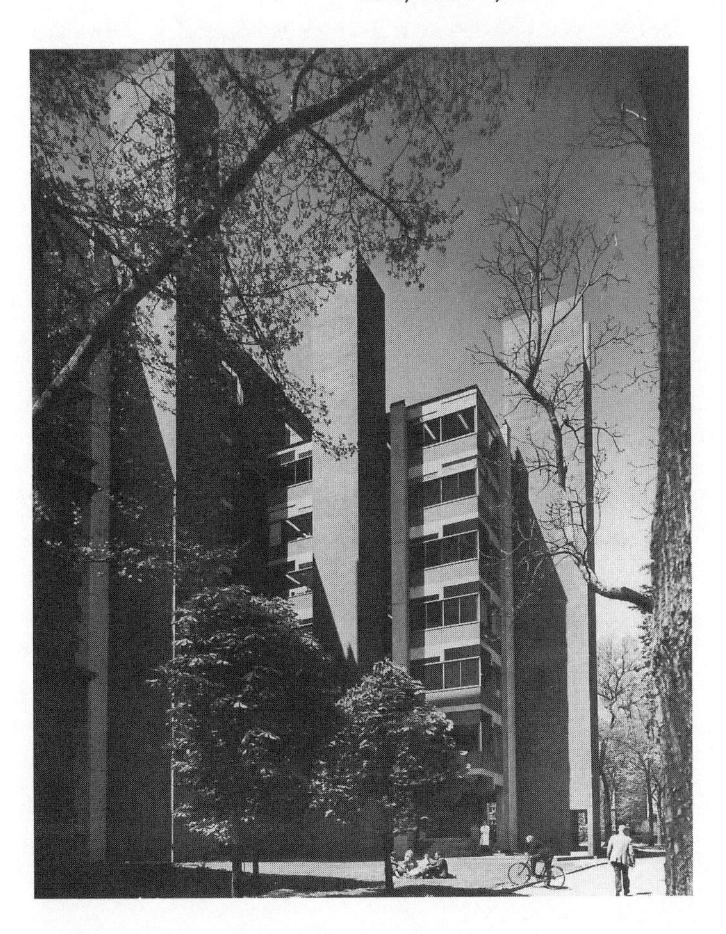

see the building a few years after it was built. My classmates and I particularly admired the exposed concrete structure and the explicit separation of what Kahn called "servant" and "served" spaces—massive brick ventilation shafts and delicate, glass-enclosed individual laboratories. However, The latter proved to be unpopular with their occupants. The large windows let in too much light (today, most are papered over with aluminum foil), cement dust from the exposed concrete beams falls on the lab tables, and the rigid plan has proved inflexible to changing needs.

The Richards Laboratory was built only 35 years ago. It is next to a student dormitory known as the Quad, a picturesque Jacobean Revival complex planned around a series of courtyards. This handsome building has been doing yeoman service for almost a century. The Quad was designed by the Philadelphia firm of Walter Cope and John Stewardson, whose work at the University of Pennsylvania, Princeton, and Bryn Mawr was largely responsible for the popularity of so-called Collegiate Gothic. Pleasing, well-loved—and well-built—the Quad is architecture of the highest order. Yet my classmates and I did not pay any attention to the dormitory when we visited Philadelphia years ago. We had never heard of Cope & Stewardson, despite their achievements and wide cultural influence. The architecture historians whom we studied—Siegfried Giedion, Nikolaus Pevs-

Fig. 2. The dormitories in the East Quad, designed by the firm Cope & Stewardson, stand next to the Richards Laboratory.

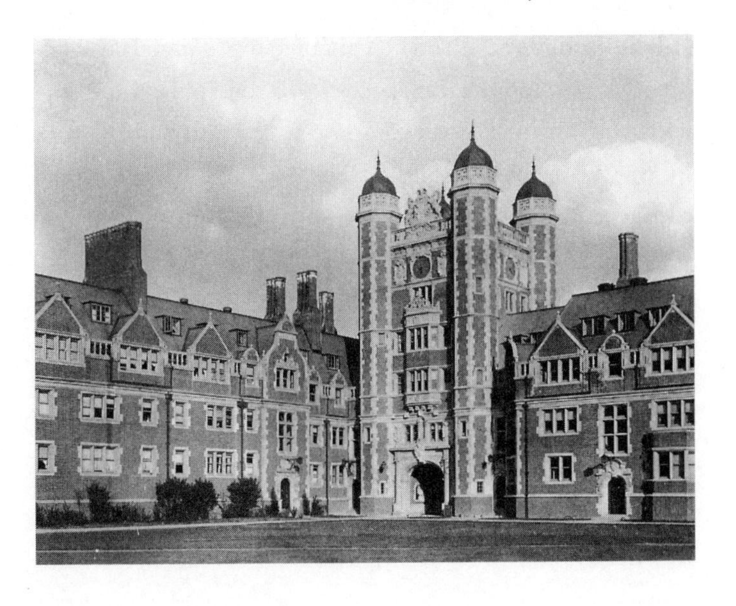

ner, James Marston Fitch—favored innovators and experimenters, even if the innovations and experiments often failed. Put another way, most historians of modern architecture gave precedence to *Delight* over *Commoditie* and *Firmeness*. This may be because the appearance of a building was easier to assess (especially at a distance) than either its functional performance or material durability. Or maybe they were attracted chiefly to the aesthetic qualities of architecture. In any case, "imaginative, inventive, and revolutionary" were more likely accolades to be showered on important buildings than "accommodating, dependable, and sound."

This is not to say that good architecture is merely utilitarian. One of the grandest spaces in Philadelphia is the concourse of Thirtieth Street Station, which was built in 1934 for the Pennsylvania Railroad by the accomplished Chicago architects Graham, Anderson, Probst & White, the successor firm of Daniel H. Burnham. The magnificent room, 290 feet long and almost 100 feet high, is covered by a flat coffered ceiling decorated in red, gold, and cream. Diffused light streams in from tall windows on both sides. Almost nothing in this memorable space—the gilded Art Deco chandeliers, the travertine walls, the massive Corinthian columns at each end—was a product of its rather mundane function: to provide a waiting space for people, before they descended the staircases that led to the platforms below. But the railroad station concourse in the heyday of railroad travel, was more than merely a place to get on and off trains. It was a gateway to the city, as well as a symbol of unreserved faith in modern transportation—and in the Pennsylvania Railroad. That is why it was appropriate for delight to take precedence over commodity.

Yet delight is not uniform. The Main Concourse of Grand Central Terminal in New York City, for example, offers different pleasures than Thirtieth Street Station. The monumental spaces are comparable in size and function. They are both well built. Similar spaces, similar materials, yet the experience of the two concourses is different. Both buildings are inspired by the Classical architecture of the past, but Grand Central, which opened in 1913, is a modified version of Beaux-Arts Classicism, whereas the Philadelphia station, despite the Corinthian columns, is simplified, abstracted, and stylized, what historians called "stripped Classicism." As a result, Grand Central is dramatic, visually rich in its details, almost Wagnerian; Thirtieth Street is equally dramatic but in a way that is coolly geometrical and sleekly urbane—not Wagner, Cole Porter. Style is evident in the smallest details. It ensures a continuity between the great vaulted sky of Grand Central and the ticket counters, or between the Thirtieth Street chandeliers and the announcement boards at each track stair. It is the visual language of a building. Architectural style is the manner in which the architect communicates a particular kind of visual delight, in large ways and small.

Commodity, firmness, and delight are never evenly weighted. Sometimes one predominates, sometimes the other. Sometimes a waiting room needs to be a triumphal celebration of arrival and departure—sometimes it is just a waiting room. Sometimes it is necessary to compromise structural simplicity to achieve an esthetic effect. Sometimes functional requirements override other considerations; a laboratory that does not serve its scientists is a failed work of architecture, no matter how beautiful its design. A banal church is a greater failure than a banal factory. The art of building requires judiciously balancing Wotton's three conditions.

The end must direct the operation. That is what distinguishes architecture from the fine arts of painting and sculpture "An artist can paint square wheels," Paul Klee once observed, "but an architect must make them round." Architecture, in this respect, is no different than other "operative arts" such as cooking. The creativity of the chef is likewise circumscribed by factors outside his control—the natural ingredients, the human palate, the chemistry of foods. The dish must be at once nourishing (commodity), cookable (firmness), and, of course, tasty (delight). (It should also look good, although the contemporary trend toward visually extravagant dishes seems to me an aberration). The art of cooking, like the art of architecture, lies in knowing how to establish the appropriate relations between the three conditions.

The experience of food is sensual. It is also first-hand. That is, while it's fun to read recipes and look at photographs of table settings in *Gourmet* magazine, no one I know considers this a substitute for eating. The experience of buildings is sensual, too. Yet, many of us get our first glimpses of buildings—particularly celebrated buildings—as images in books, magazines, newspapers, public lectures, and exhibitions. One of the most famous buildings of the Modern movement, Ludwig Mies van der Rohe's Barcelona Pavilion, was known almost entirely through photographs since it was built for an exhibition that lasted only seven months. Before photography, the Paimio Tubercolosis Sanatorium, located in a remote part of Finland, would have remained obscure; as it was, its stunning images brought the young Alvar Aalto worldwide recognition. The Sydney Opera House is another world-famous building that, at least outside Australia, relatively few people have seen first-hand. Yet photography tells us very little about how a building fulfills its function, or about how it is built. For example, the handrails in the often-photographed stairway of the Paimio sanatorium look like standard International Style metal pipes. In fact they are wood—much more pleasant to the touch—painted to look like metal. Well-known photographs of the Barcelona Pavilion show eight free-standing columns supporting a flat slab, and free-standing marble screens that carry no loads, a prototypical International Style structure. In reality, there are columns concealed within the screens, which are not slabs of marble but thin marble sheets attached to a masonry back-up wall. In other words, this 1929 building is an example of traditional layered construction, not of modernistic structural purism.[1]

In photographs, buildings are forever young. The ravages of time, weather, and use are banished. It is a shock to come across a revered architectural icon and to find the concrete stained, the painted window frames chipped, the tiles cracked. Of course, all buildings age, but some age more gracefully than others. A 450-year-old Palladio villa retains its beauty, despite peeling plaster and mossy stonework (perhaps it even looks more enchanting). Most modern buildings, on the other hand, lose their potency if they are not gleaming and machinelike.

Obviously, photography highlights the visual qualities of buildings and ignores commodity and firmness. Yet photography cannot completely communicate delight. A visitor to the Seagram Building in New York, for example, is surprised to discover the subtle relationship between Mies' bronze tower and the Italian Renaissance façade of McKim, Mead & White's Racquet and Tennis Club on the other side of Park Avenue. Equally deceptive are photographs of Frank Lloyd Wright's work in Oak Park, since they give no hint of the comfortable suburban surroundings of his so-called prairie houses. As I student, I studied the buildings of Le Corbusier in black and white photographs, which did not prepare me for the shock of experiencing his often wildly polychrome interiors. Nor can photography communicate movement, which is such an integral part of the architectural experience (film is better at this, but not much). Nothing conveys the actual experience of a building like the real thing. To paraphrase Robert Hughes, a photograph of architecture is to architecture as telephone sex is to sex.

Never is modern architectural photography more misleading than in its portrayal of domestic interiors. Interiors are usually photographed empty or with minimal furnishings, before the owners have had the opportunity to move in and (presumably) defile the purity of the design. But even if the space is occupied, strict conventions prevail: furniture must be lined up just so; there must be no distractions, no half-empty tea cups, no crumpled newspapers, no abandoned children's toys. Books on shelves are arranged to create interesting patterns, personal mementos are temporarily banished—everything must be neat. I once observed a photographer's assistant during a photo shoot comb out the fringe of a rug. Such primping and visual editing sets off the architecture to best advantage. It also—not coincidentally—gives the impression that the designed interior is autonomous and self-contained: in other words, that it is a work of art. Markedly, these photographs never include human figures. People would be the greatest distraction of all.

The world of buildings depicted in books and magazines is a scaleless, self-sufficient place. The absence of people in architectural photographs has several effects. In the past, the proportions and dimensions of buildings were based on the human body. While this was done for philosophical reasons, it also ensured a direct relationship between architecture and people—it is why even very large Classical buildings feel comfortable. By removing people from buildings, architectural photography makes it possible to regard architecture as an abstraction, unrelated to humans. It is not merely that the conventions of modern architectural photography ideally communicate the intentions of most modern architects, it is also that they validate those intentions. People? Who needs them?

While I was writing *Home*, I discovered that the most useful historical sources for information about how people furnished and decorated their homes were often paintings. Not paintings in which the room was the subject, but portraits and domestic genre scenes. An example of the latter is James Tissot's, "Hide and Seek," which shows four little girls at play in a Victorian sitting room. The décor is exotic, an eclectic mixture of Persian rugs, Chinese porcelain pots, and tiger-skins and others furs scattered over the furniture.

Tissot was a French painter who settled in London in 1871. An easel in the corner suggests that this is his own house, in which case, the woman sunk deep into an easy chair, reading a newspaper may be his Irish mistress. John Singer Sargent's masterpiece, "The Daughters of Edward Darley Boit," painted in 1882, likewise shows four girls. Henry James described it as "the happy play-world of a family of charming children," but the girls can hardly be said to be playing. Properly dressed in white pinafores, black socks, and patent leather shoes, they form a motionless tableau. The room, in an apartment in Paris, is stylishly bare, unadorned except for two immense Japanese vases and a red screen. The mood is entirely different in the Swedish painter Carl Larsson's playful "Mother's and the Cherubs' Room," which was included in Larsson's famous book *Ett Hem* (At Home), published in 1899. The walls of his wife's

Fig. 3. James Tissot's "Hide and Seek," a scene of domestic life painted circa 1880-1882.

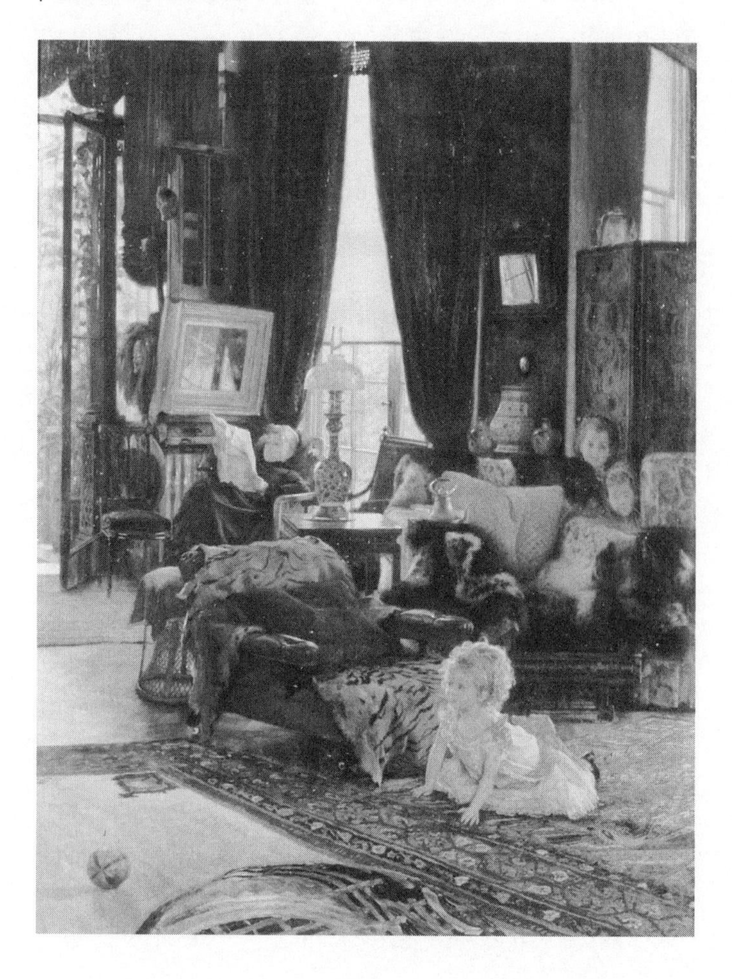

bedroom are wooden boards, whitewashed and decorated with a painted frieze of ribboned garlands; the ceiling, likewise wood, is painted green with red trim. The simple furniture is also painted in bright colors. Karin Larsson's bed is separated from the children's cots by a striped woven curtain. We see three of the Larsson girls in various stages of dress—and undress. That is appropriate, too, for naturalism and artlessness permeate this charming scene.

Such paintings are more faithful depictions of domestic surroundings than modern architectural photographs. For one thing, they are full of the signs of everyday life. A coat is thrown casually over a chair, there are crumbs on the table, Tissot's little girl playing on the floor rumples the carpet. Moreover, in these interiors the architecture is in the background. It is a setting for human activity—just as it is in real life. Paintings also convey something about the *atmosphere* of the interior. Dutch seventeenth-century domestic paintings, for example, exude a prosperous air of bourgeois comfort and propriety. A hundred years later, François Boucher painted a middle-class French family gathering for morning coffee in a little room with japanned woodwork and gilded moldings. There is a sweet intimacy here that is absent in the Dutch interiors. An interior of the same period by Henry Walton shows an English gentleman at breakfast. He is sitting in a relaxed posture, wearing a rid-

Fig. 4 (RIGHT). François Boucher's portrait of French middle-class life, "Coffee in the Closet," 1739.

Fig. 5 (BELOW). "An English Gentleman at Breakfast" by Henry Walton, 1775—a moment of domestic repose.

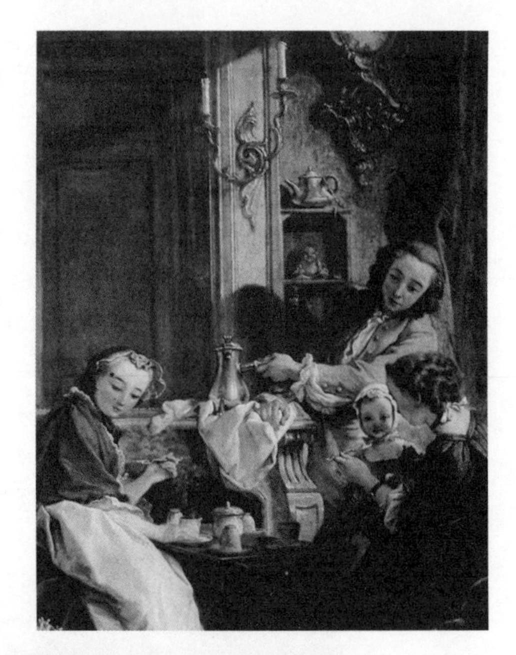

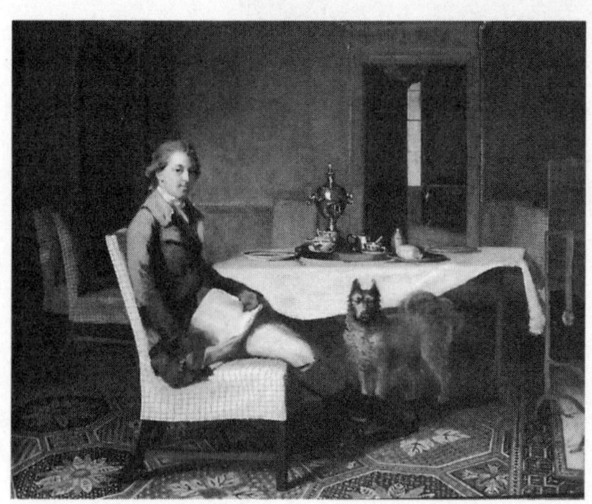

ing-coat and boots, accompanied by his dog. The ambience is one of informal and relaxed country life.

As I studied such paintings, I started to see associations between the rooms and their inhabitants. The legs of the mahogany furniture in an English country house were as straight and unadorned as their owners' riding boots. The arabesques and curlicues of the moldings and architectural ornaments in a French salon mirrored the flouncing ribbons that adorned the women's dresses and the frills of the men's shirts. The proper black broadcloth and white lace collars of the Dutch men and women echoed the spotless black-and-white checkerboard marble floors. I became convinced that a strong connection exists between the way that we decorate our homes and the way that we dress ourselves.

There are three distinct reasons for the intimate relationship between dress and décor. The first is technical. Décor, like dress, incorporates fabrics. Curtains, swags, and window-treatments are made of silk, damask, satin, brocade, wool, muslin, and velvet—so is clothing. Woven materials are used in tapestries, wall-hangings, carpets and upholstery as well as coats and skirts. Inevitably, the dressmaker's techniques of embroidering, gathering, pleating, and trimming find their way into décor. This is why furniture skirts recall women's skirts, and why the fringes, cords, and bobbins of nineteenth-century drapery recall ladies' ballgowns. The delicate lace curtains and the billowing baldachin over a bed in a ladies' boudoir matched the clothes in her dressing room.

The connection between décor and dress can be even more intimate, for architecture sometimes directly mimics dress. The garlands in eighteenth-century buildings are sculpted or painted versions of the sashes and flowered ornaments worn by men and women. The ancient Greeks incorporated elements of dress in temple architecture. This is most apparent in colonnades, which Vincent Scully has likened to hoplites massed in a phalanx.[2] There is no doubt that Classical columns were given human attributes. Ancient authors likened the vertical flutes to the folds in a chiton, or tunic.[3] Columns have capitals—that is, heads. The moldings of Doric capitals were sometimes painted to resemble headbands; Ionic and Corinthian capitals incorporated carved head garlands, and the curving tendrils of Corinthian capitals often look more like hair than foliage. Indeed, Vitruvius considered the Corinthian order "feminine," as opposed to the sturdy masculine Doric. Sir Henry Wotton went so far as to call the Corinthian order "lascivious" and "decked like a wanton courtesan."[4]

The second connection between dress and décor is social. In the 1890s, the famous English economist Alfred Marshall observed that as people earned more money, they

Fig. 6. The Corinthian order, "decked like a wanton courtesan," in the opinion of Sir Henry Wotton.

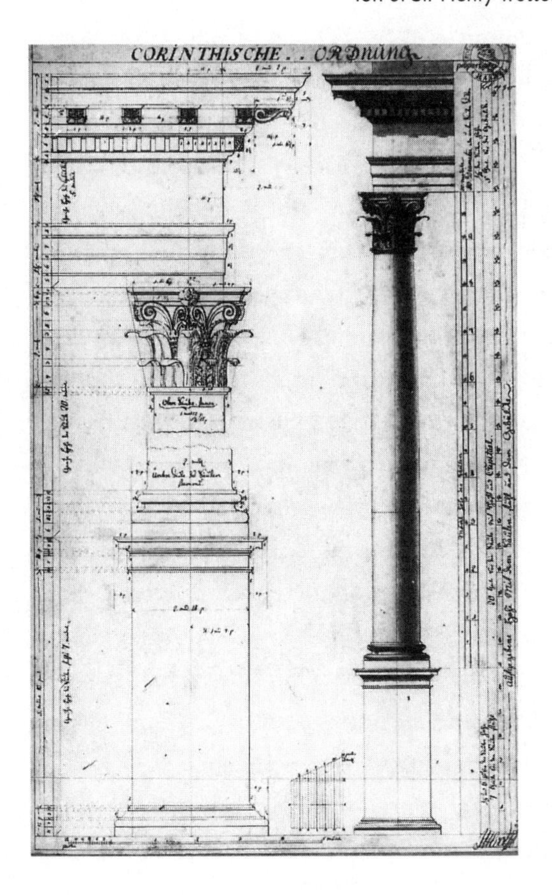

wanted better food, better clothes and larger homes—both for social standing and comfort. Since homes and clothes are timeworn ways in which to convey status, there is a conformity in the types of materials and symbols used to convey social standing. If family coats of arms are displayed, they will be seen on wall medallions as well as on blazer buttons. If gold is treasured, the wealthy will wear gold braid and surround themselves with gilt moldings. If this is considered too flashy, other materials can convey status: stainless steel kitchen appliances and stainless steel watch bracelets. Diamonds may be forever, but fashions change. Today, leather is considered a luxury material, and is used both for expensive clothing and expensive sofas. A hundred years ago, leather was considered utilitarian; leather aprons and vests were worn only by workmen, and leather easy chairs were only found in smoking rooms and men's clubs since leather was less flammable than fabric. But it was never used in salons or drawing rooms. When corduroy, originally used only in workingmen's dress, became accepted by the middle class, it also showed up as upholstery. The current fashion for "natural" dress fabrics—cotton, wool, linen—has a counterpart in "natural" décor: exposed brick, oiled wood, polished concrete.

In a more general sense—and this has nothing to do with conspicuous consumption—both homes and clothes convey values. Carl Larsson's home was a statement of both his and Karin's naturalistic aesthetic ideals, so was James Tissot's exotic sitting room. Whether or not we are artists, our homes, like our clothes, communicate who we are, or at least how we wish others to perceive us: starchly formal or comfortably casual, intensely avant-garde or resolutely traditional, bohemian or conservative, cosmopolitan or down-home. The Che Guevara poster on the wall and the embroidered denim jacket convey one set of values; Colonial break-fronts and penny loafers, another. That is why it is disconcerting if dress and décor are not in harmony. Sweat shirts and running shoes in a Louis Quinze drawing room send a decidedly mixed message, as does a three-piece suit on the deck of a Malibu beach bungalow.

The third connection between dress and décor concerns perception. Architecture, interior decoration, and fashion design are three distinct fields, yet we experience them with the same eye. Whether we look at dress or décor, we bring the same visual bias, the same sensibility, the same taste. This sensibility is not constant. Sometimes we appreciate simplicity, sometimes complexity. Fashionable seventeenth-century French eyes, for example, favored floral decorations and embroidery, and introduced the custom of having vases of fresh flowers in the home. English eyes in the midst of the Neoclassic revival sought fundamental simplicity and sobriety in men's clothes as well as in architecture. Victorian eyes fancied dense patterns that were likely to show up in waistcoats and on wainscotting. Parisian eyes, in the early 1900s, admired the same neo-*Empire* motifs in dress and décor.*

Early twentieth-century eyes had their own particular sensibility. One of the great interiors of this period is the main living space of the Tugendhat House, designed by Mies Van der Rohe in 1928. The house stands outside Brno, Czechoslovakia. The exterior is a low-key International Style white box, but the interior is astonishing. The public rooms are contained in one large open space. A curved wall of macassar ebony defines the dining room, and a straight free-standing wall of onyx dorée separates the music room from the living room. The space is punctuated by slender cruciform columns covered in chromed metal. The east and south walls are floor-to-ceiling glass—a precursor of Mies' famous glass house. The sense of openness is heightened when, at the touch of a button, fifteen-foot sections of the glass wall sink into the ground.

I have never seen the Tugendhat House, except in a handful of black-and-white photographs (the house was

*The celebrated couturier Paul Poiret, anticipating Ralph Lauren, opened an interior decorating shop named "Martine" in 1911.

severely damaged during the Second World War). This is another case where photographs are a poor substitute. They do not convey the rich textures of the raw silk and velvet draperies, nor the vivid colors of the upholstery: emerald green leather and ruby-red velvet. Nor do they capture the sumptuous range of materials: onyx, pearwood, handwoven wool, chromed metal and (surprisingly) a linoleum floor. Since the surviving photographs do not show any human figures, they heighten the impression that the house was built yesterday, especially as the furniture, designed by the architect, is still in production.

Mies van der Rohe appears in a photograph taken in 1926. The place is Stuttgart, the site of the famous Weissenhof housing exhibition, which he planned, and where he brought together the leading exponents of the soon-to-be-christened International Style. One of these was Le Corbusier, who is also in the photograph. The two firebrands, who will soon set the architectural world on its ear, are deep in conversation. Le Corbusier smokes a pipe and sports a jaunty derby and a loose, short tweed coat. Mies, looking older than his forty years, wears a Homburg, a long dark ulster, and spats. This photograph puts the Tugendhat House in context. However "modern" the airy room appears to my eyes, it contained a considered and formal way of life that is as remote from me as waxed moustaches, Homburgs,

Fig. 7 (BELOW). Mies van der Rohe, in a Homburg, ulster, and spats, and Le Corbusier, with a pipe and derby, Stuttgart, 1926.

Fig. 8 (OPPOSITE PAGE, TOP). The elegant public rooms of Mies van der Rohe's Tugendhat House, 1928.

Fig. 9 (OPPOSITE PAGE, BOTTOM). Where Mies van der Rohe is formal, Charles Moore is casual, in this house built for himself in 1962.

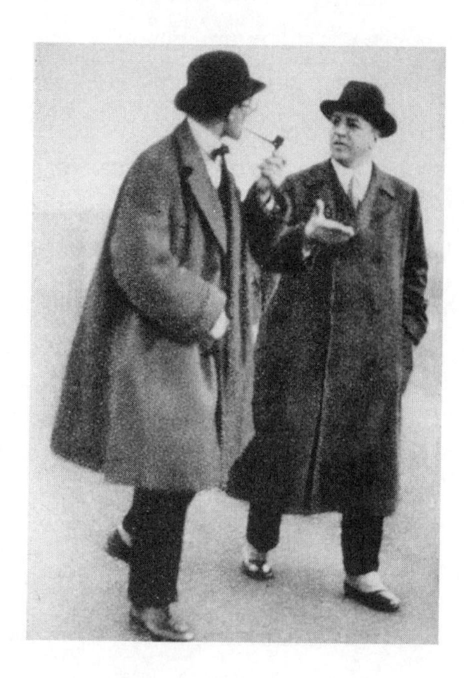

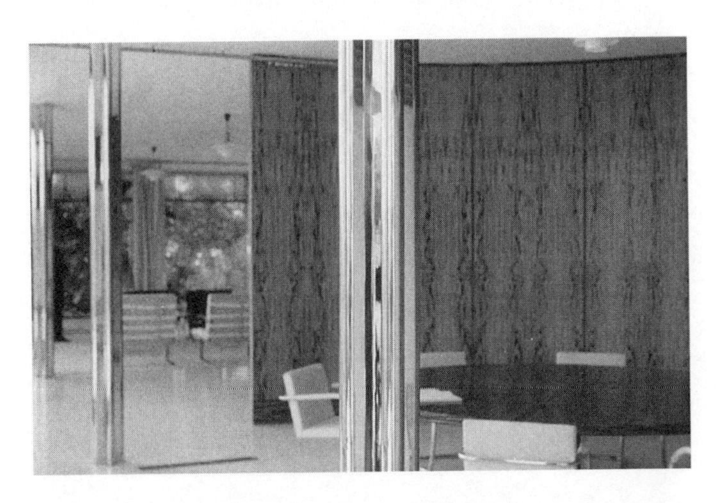

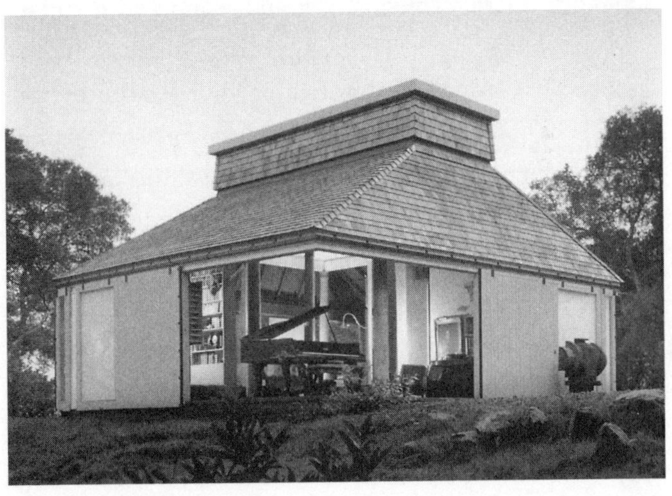

and spats. It is in that context that Mies' curious combination of ordered simplicity and sybaritic luxury must be understood.

Nothing could be less similar to the Tugendhat House than Charles Moore's weekend house that he built for himself in the hills above Berkeley, California. I saw it in the summer of 1964, two years after it was built. While the Tugendhat House appears sexy and glamorous, the Moore house is at first glance downright rustic, a little barn, twenty-six feet square, capped by a saddle roof. It is an elegant little barn, however, with white-painted walls and large windows that open up the corners, not by disappearing into the ground but by sliding sideways like barn doors. The one-room interior contains a grand piano and a sunken bath that looks vaguely Roman, perhaps because the skylight above it is supported by four solid fir Tuscan columns (found by Moore at a demolition site). Four similar columns support a second skylight over a sitting area.

I admire the Tugendhat House, but I could not imagine living in it. That is, I could not imagine having to dress up sufficiently to feel at home. The Moore house, on the other hand, reflects a more compliant sensibility. Its floor-to-ceiling windows, spare detailing, and open interior mark it as a successor to the International Style. Yet the shingled roof and the Tuscan columns hearken back to older traditions. The little building manages to be comfortable, relaxed, archetypal, and vaguely ironic, all at the same time. The eclectic, Californian setting is both informal and formal. Put another way, it is a place where people who wear tweed jackets with jeans, or silk skirts with canvas espadrilles would fit right in.

The little Moore barn is an historic building. Together with Robert Venturi's Vanna Venturi House, which was designed the same year, it marks the advent of an architectural style that became known as Postmodernism.[5] One of the celebrated buildings of Postmodernism is James Stirling's Neue Staatsgalerie in Stuttgart, which was completed in 1984. Stirling vastly expands Moore's eclecticism, combining a bewildering mixture of forms; a Doric portico, a staid neoclassical wing that matches the existing museum, an Egyptian-looking curved cornice, a colorful Russian Constructivist entrance canopy, a curving steel-and-glass wall, and two huge blue ventilator funnels lifted straight from the Centre Georges Pompidou. The monumental façade of alternating bands of travertine and sandstone is undermined by oversized fiberglass handrails that look like pink sausages. I couldn't understand this design, except as a tour-de-force, until I visited the building. It was a wintry Sunday, and the Staatsgalerie was packed—it is one of the most popular museums in Germany. Now the architecture made

Fig. 10. James Stirling's Neue Staatsgalerie in Stuttgart. The eclectic design attracts a variety of visitors.

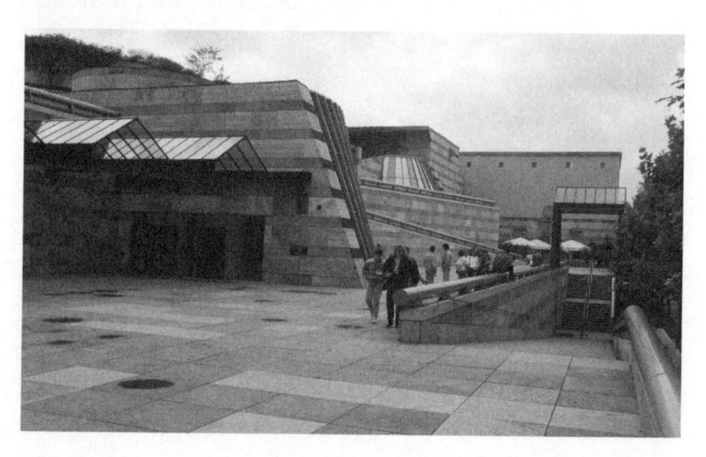

sense. This museum-cum-discotheque was the perfect setting for the eclectic crowd. We were wearing every type of dress imaginable: casual wear, business suits, ski parkas, work clothes. Some people dressed up for a Sunday visit to the museum, some dressed down. Stirling's lively collage absorbed us all. I did not see any gentlemen in Homburgs and spats, but they would have fitted in, too.

A number of years ago I accompanied the architect Jack Diamond on a visit to a building that he had just completed at York University in Toronto. It was a student center, containing a food court and lounges on the main level and student organization offices on the second floor. The exterior of the building was decidedly traditional. Facing a landscaped common, the well-proportioned façade consisted of a colonnaded brick base supporting a row of double columns capped by a deep copper-lined cornice. Behind the colonnade, which was fitted with retractable glass panels that could be opened during warm weather, was a two-story-high hall lit by three large skylights. The exterior had a simplicity that reminded me of McKim, Mead & White, albeit without Classical ornament.

The interior was different, with many hallmarks of the International Style: no decoration, bare concrete, exposed structural beams, factory sash glazing and steel pipe railings. I assumed that the stark simplicity was the result of a restricted budget, and a desire to use materials that would withstand wear and tear. It seemed pretty banal to me, and although I didn't say anything to Jack, I was disappointed. Yet as we walked around, I changed my mind. Although the décor was tough and unsentimental, it was not crude. There were sleek stainless-steel pendant lighting fixtures with suspended glass diffusers and stylish easy chairs covered in canvas. In the food court, the bar and counter tops were marble, the dining tables solid maple. Students were gathered around tables, lounging on the staircase, sprawled on the floor. The atmosphere was hard to pin down. This was not the precious, corporate modernism of Richard Meier, nor the contrived, technological wizardry of Norman Foster. It was certainly not the Calvinist minimalism that I associated with many trendy younger architects. I couldn't put my finger on it until I realized that the functional but chic décor reminded me of the no-nonsense styling of a Benetton clothing store.

I happen to like Collegiate Gothic buildings. I like their dark rooms with wood paneling, hammer-beam ceilings, and traditional oak furniture. But seeing the York student center made me realize that whenever I walk through these old buildings I also experience a nagging dissatisfaction. It has to do with the students. The young men and women in baseball caps, shorts, stenciled sweat shirts, and iridescent nylon windbreakers just don't fit in. They should be wearing boaters and blazers, tweeds and flannels. Of course, no student that I have ever seen—including at Oxford—dresses that way. I may deplore the loss of decorum, but as an architect I can't do anything to change it. It is the building that must do the accommodating.

If the relationship between dress and décor is intimate, it is also one-sided. Interior decorators and architects will bridle at this, but there is no doubt that dress comes first. "People have always worn what they wanted to wear," writes Anne Hollander, "fashion exists to keep fulfilling that desire."[6] And architecture must follow. For the truth is that a building—no matter how useful or well built or beautiful—that is not sympathetic to the way that people dress risks looking not merely anachronistic, but downright silly. Like it or not, architecture cannot escape fashion.

TWO
IN AND OUT OF FASHION

Bryant Park, in midtown Manhattan, is the site of a biannual fashion show. Twice a year, in large white tents crammed with reporters, photographers, editors, and celebrity guests, models parade designers' wares on the runway. Bryant Park is also a good place to observe an architectural fashion show. A row of Twenties beauties lines 40th Street, along the south side of the park. First is Ely Jacques Kahn's French Renaissance office building, originally the headquarters of *Scientific American*. Its neighbor is the stately Classical Engineers Club. Then comes a flapper, Raymond Hood's American Radiator Building, whose black brick and gold trim sets it apart from its neighbors. Charles Rich's Bryant Park Studios, an elegant survivor of the late Gilded Age, is at the Sixth Avenue corner. The large north-facing windows and glazed penthouse are

Fig. 11. The group of buildings to the south of Bryant Park and the New York Public Library along 40th Street. The black American Radiator Building stands out in the center.

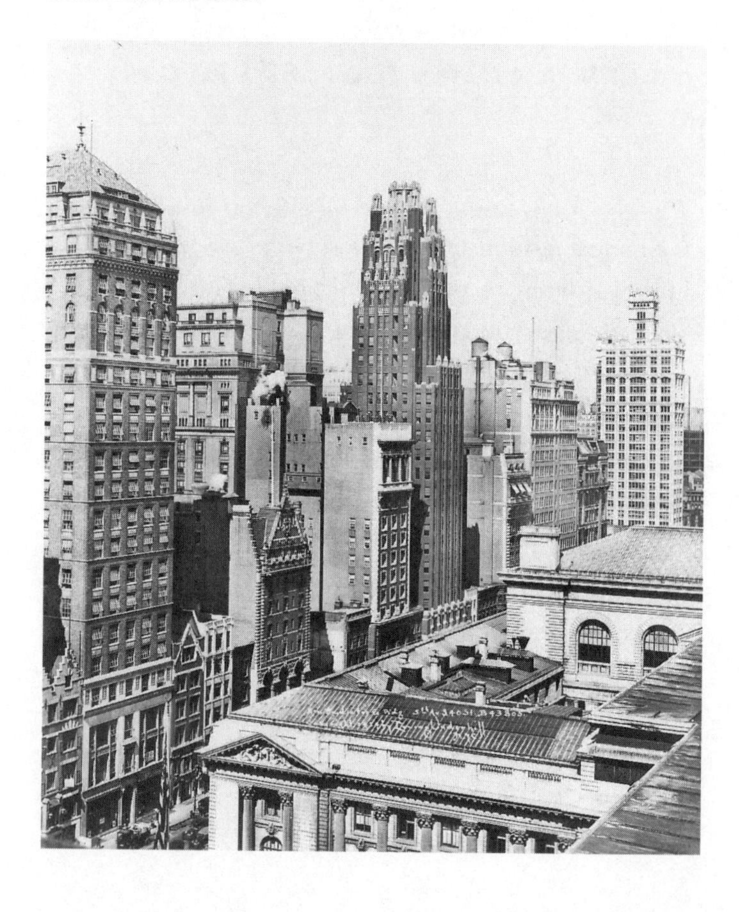

a reminder that this building was originally intended for artists.

Bryant Park Studios is built in an architectural style that was originally called Modern French but today is commonly referred to as Beaux-Arts, in recognition of the influential Ecole des Beaux-Arts in Paris. Starting with Richard Morris Hunt, during the second half of the nineteenth century many of the best American architects were graduates of the Ecole. H. H. Richardson and his protégé Charles Follen McKim were alumni, as well as McKim's assistants, John M. Carrère and Thomas Hastings. Carrère and Hastings were the architects of the New York Public Library, whose stately presence commands the east side of Bryant Park. Narrow strips of windows indicate the book-stacks, above them nine thermal windows signal the vast reading room. In typical Beaux-Arts fashion, the façade manages to appear both grandly monumental and coolly rational, except for a curious row of little doorways high up the wall, which lack balconies or even railings and open into mid-air. The strange little sky-exits, which a friend who works at the library claims are for staff defenestration, provide a fanciful note to the great marble façade.*

*I have been unable to ascertain the function of these doorways. They are operable, but the explanation that they were intended for ventilation, or to accommodate a future expansion, is unconvincing.

A row of no-nonsense 1970s office blocks lines Sixth Avenue on the west side of the park. The largest is the New York Telephone Company Building, whose banal façade of gray-tinted glass and vertical strips of marble fills the block between 41st and 42nd Street. The north side of the park is dominated by the fifty-story W. R. Grace Building, designed by Gordon Bunshaft of Skidmore, Owings & Merrill in 1972. The swooping travertine façade appears to have been inspired by the buildings of Brasília. This bit of tropical flash is flanked by an undistinguished mirrored glass tower, and a generic brick-and-Colonial-trim box. Built 50 years apart, these commercial office blocks share a balefully functionalist approach to architecture. They are strictly off-the-rack buildings that only a developer could love.

Bryant Park also offers distant views of two of Manhattan's most distinctive skyscrapers: the Chrysler Building and the Empire State Building. The Chrysler Building started life as a speculative office building. In 1927, the architect William Van Alen, influenced by the recent Parisian exhibition of the *arts décoratifs,* designed a skyscraper in a style that has come to be known as Art Deco. When the plans were finished, but before construction had begun, the design and the building site were bought by the automobile magnate Walter P. Chrysler. Chrysler wanted the building to serve as a billboard for his company. Van Alen obligingly grafted on

Fig. 12 (BELOW). The Chrysler Building, once derisively labeled "a stunt design," is now considered an Art Deco masterpiece.

Fig. 13 (RIGHT). The Empire State Building. The spire, topped by a broadcast antenna, was originally designed as a mooring station for dirigibles.

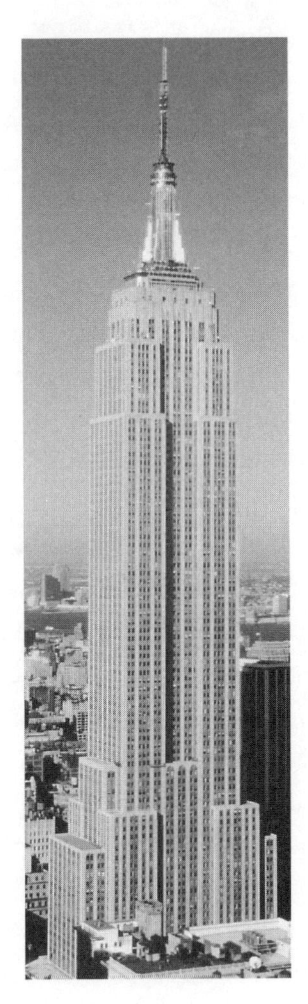

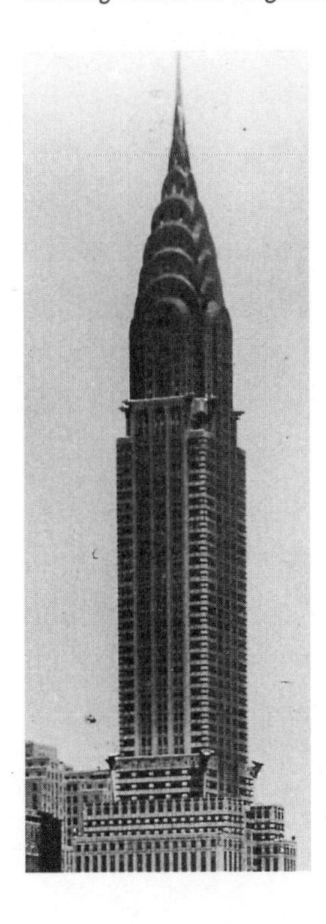

eagle-head gargoyles (based on hood ornaments), winged radiator caps, a frieze of steel hubcaps, and black brick accents that suggest running boards. The tower's most distinctive feature was its stainless-steel cap, which held the Cloud Club, a private dining room for Chrysler executives. Today, the flamboyant Chrysler Building is considered a brilliant emblem of the Jazz Age, but it was not an instant success. When it was built it was roundly criticized as frivolous and flashy. "A stunt design," sniffed *The New Yorker*. The *New York Times* likewise derided the blatant commercialism of the architecture.

The Chrysler Building had the distinction of being the world's tallest building—for a few months, until it was surpassed by the Empire State Building. Although designed at the same time as the Chrysler, the Empire State is quite different in appearance. Its exterior is the architectural equivalent of a gray flannel suit. There is no decoration. The plain limestone walls lack even traditional cornices; chrome-nickel steel mullions extend uninterrupted from the 6th to the 85th floor, accentuating the building's height. "Ornament is crime" Adolf Loos had proclaimed years before, but the stripped-down appearance of the Empire State Building owed more to an accelerated building schedule—construction took less than eighteen months—than to architectural ideology. In fact, the architects of the skyscraper considered themselves traditionalists. Richmond H. Shreve worked for Carrère & Hastings on the New York Public Library, where he met William Lamb, a recent Ecole graduate. After Carrère's unfortunate death in an auto accident and Hastings' retirement, Shreve and Lamb took over the firm (for several years it was called Carrère & Hastings, Shreve & Lamb) and were eventually joined by Arthur Loomis Harmon, who had worked for McKim, Mead & White on the Metropolitan Museum of Art. Despite—or rather because of—their solid Classical roots, Shreve, Lamb and Harmon designed a beautifully proportioned building that became the most famous skyscraper in the world.

The Empire State Building has one whimsical touch. The final plans called for the skyscraper to end with a flat roof over the 85th floor—1,050 feet, precisely calculated to be two feet higher than the top of the Chrysler Building's spire. Then, before construction began, the owners decided that two feet was not enough, and ordered the architects to add a 200-foot tower to the top of the building.* This was to be not merely a decorative spire but a functioning symbol of the modern age, a mooring tower for airships. Instead of dropping transatlantic travelers off at Lakehurst, N.J., the

*At 1,250 feet—the equivalent of 102 floors—the Empire State remained the world's tallest building until the construction of the World Trade Center towers in 1972.

thousand-foot-long dirigibles would fly right into Manhattan and hook themselves up to the top of the Empire State Building. Passengers would disembark to an observation platform and descend by elevator to a lounge and customs area on the 86th floor. Most experts, including Hugo Eckener, commander of the *Graf Zeppelin*, doubted that it could be done. It was hard enough to dock the unwieldy leviathans at ground level, never mind 1,250 feet up in the air. The experts proved to be right, and no airship passengers ever landed atop the Empire State.[1] Yet the rocket-shaped tower, with its cast aluminum buttresses and gleaming conical top, is the perfect fanciful crown for this rather solemn skyscraper.

Whimsy is absent from the tops of the 1970s office blocks around Bryant Park. They look as if the architects had lopped them off on a whim: "I can do 40 floors, or 42, or 45. Just tell me when to stop." More recent skyscrapers around Bryant Park, no doubt emboldened by Philip Johnson's Chippendale top on his AT&T Building, have more animated crowns. The hipped roof of a Fifth Avenue Post-modern high-rise adorned with circles and squares peeks out above the library. The top of the Bertelsmann Building is a slender spike. The new Condé Nast office tower has tilted forms resembling speaker cabinets on its roof. Pretty tame stuff compared to the more fanciful crowns of the

1920s buildings—neo-Gothic spires, Romanesque tile roofs, copper domes. The 58 floors of 500 Fifth Avenue (at the corner of Fifth Avenue and 42nd Street), which was designed by Shreve & Lamb prior to the Empire State Building, step back dramatically as they reach the building's apex. Spiky, wrought-iron finials enliven the chateau-like roof of the Scientific American Building. An animated silhouette of black brick with gilded and red highlights crowns the Radiator Building. According to Hood, the dramatic effect (floodlit at night) suggested a "pile of coal, glowing at the top."

Raymond M. Hood was the outstanding commercial architect of the 1920s. He and John Mead Howells won a celebrated international architectural competition for the Chicago Tribune tower in Chicago with a handsome Gothic design based on the Butter Tower of Rouen Cathedral. The Chicago Tribune competition led to several New York commissions, including the Radiator Building, the Daily News Building, and the McGraw-Hill Building. With these designs, Hood developed the distinctly American approach to skyscrapers that would influence Van Alen and a generation of skyscraper designers: tall buildings conceived as Nietzschean symbols of corporate power or, to put it more mundanely, architecture as advertising. Hood once pointed out that since modern office buildings would be amortized

Fig. 14 (LEFT). Raymond Hood and John Mead Howells' Chicago Tribune Tower, the last Gothic skyscraper, beat International Style designs in a controversial building competition.

Fig. 15 (RIGHT). The 70-story RCA Building, the centerpiece of Rockefeller Center.

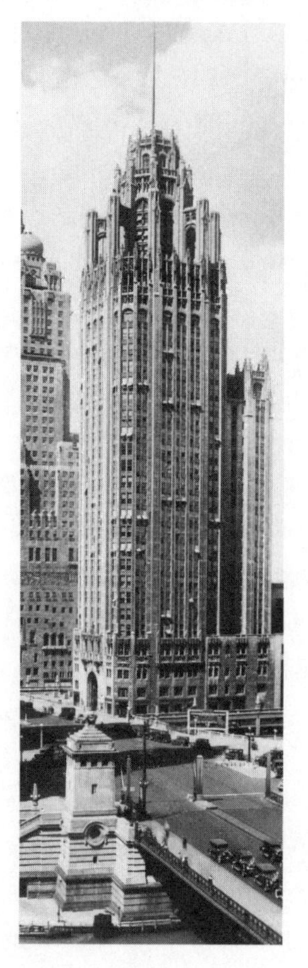

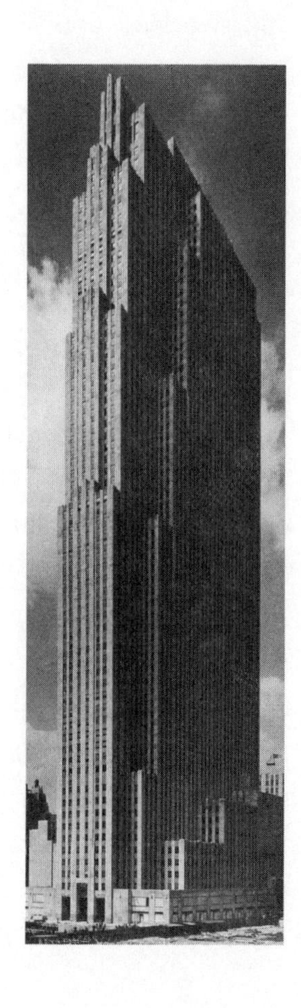

in only 20 years, architects had an opportunity to experiment. The Daily News is a robust pinnacle, with alternating vertical strips of masonry and glass. His final skyscraper, the McGraw-Hill Building, is a witty blue-green take on the International Style, complete with the company's name in huge "Broadway" style lettering on the top. Hood was also one of the key designers in the team of architects responsible for Rockefeller Center. His influence is felt in the centerpiece tower, the 70-story cliff-like RCA Building. This twentieth-century abstracted version of medieval verticality is one of New York's most evocative skyscrapers, unsurpassed since it was completed in 1934.

Bryant Park chronicles a hundred years of changing architectural fashions. Buildings are sometimes referred to as *timeless*, as if this were the highest praise one could bestow. That is nonsense. The best buildings, like the Chrysler or the New York Public Library or the RCA, are precisely *of* their time. That is part of the pleasure of looking at buildings from the past. They reflect old values and bygone virtues and vices: the self-confidence of the library, the cheerful boosterism of Chrysler, the sobriety of RCA. Even the bland goofiness of the Grace Building recalls the naïve optimism of an earlier era. That is why old buildings are precious, that is why we fight to preserve them. It is not only because we think them beautiful, or significant. It is also because they remind us of who we once were. And of who we might be again, for old buildings also inspire. The ruins of ancient Rome inspired the Renaissance architects. The palazzos of Renaissance Italy inspired Charles McKim. And the memory of McKim's Pennsylvania Station inspired David Childs of Skidmore, Owings & Merrill to transform McKim's old Post Office Building into a projected railroad terminal for the city.

Sometimes old buildings inspire us, sometimes the opposite is true. We look at an old building and ask ourselves, "What on earth were those people thinking of?" I cannot warm to heroic public buildings of the 1960s, for example. It is more than 35 years since Lincoln Center was built, enough time for the buildings to mellow, yet I can't summon any sympathy for the colonnaded brutes. The idea of putting three theaters under one roof must have been compelling at one time, but when I visit the Kennedy Center in Washington, D.C., all I see are miles of red carpeting in those Brobdingnagian lobbies. Yet, who knows? Perhaps one day a future generation will see something in these buildings that eludes me.

The Kennedy Center was criticized from the start, but the dazzling décor of Radio City Music Hall, which opened in 1932—in the midst of the Depression—guaranteed its

Fig. 16. The stage of Radio City Music Hall, opened in 1932, has been considered in turn opulent, kitschy, and a classic.

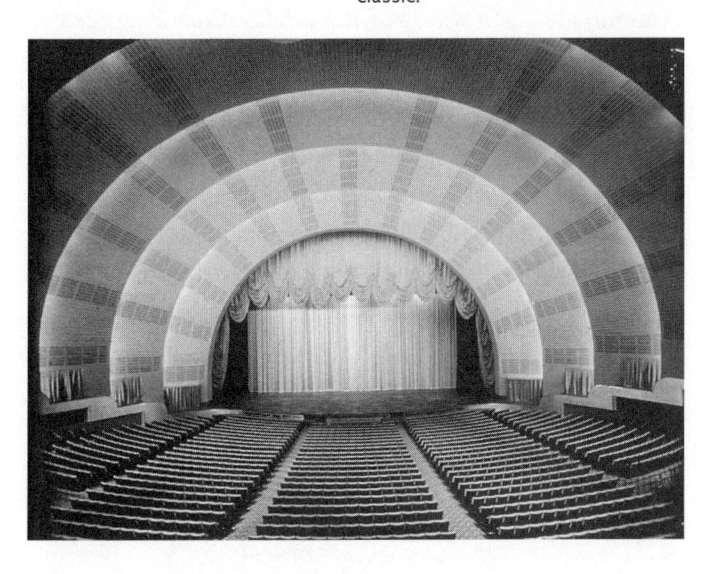

immediate success. Radio City became the most famous theater in the country, the Rockettes the most famous chorus line, "live from Radio City" the most famous dateline. In the late 1950s, when I visited New York City as a boy with my parents, Radio City was still one of the obligatory tourist sites. What I don't remember is ever learning about Radio City as an architecture student. According to the reductive standards of my International Style teachers, its opulent materials, its glowing colors, and its very theatricality disqualified Radio City as architecture (never mind that it was a technologically sophisticated "machine for entertainment"). It was dismissed as kitsch. By 1978, Radio City had lost its glamour, and the owners of Rockefeller Center decided to demolish the aging hall. Thanks to preservationists' efforts, the hall was saved from demolition and granted landmark status. Now, 20 years later, freshened by a masterful restoration, it is once again acclaimed as a masterpiece.

Radio City Music Hall is a reminder that it is not buildings that change, but architectural fashions. What seemed exciting in one decade, looks gaudy, if not downright embarrassing, in the next—or simply boring. When old buildings are torn down, the motive may be expediency or crass commercialism, but it may also be a desire for something new. This is as true of buildings as it is of women's hats, *pace* Le Corbusier.

• • •

Fashion has increasingly—and restrictively—become a term used in connection with women's dress, as in "fashion designer" or "the fashion industry." The Oxford English Dictionary defines fashion more broadly as "the mode of dress, etiquette, furniture, style of speech, etc., adopted in a society for the time being." People have to cut their hair, eat, clothe themselves, decorate their homes—fashion affects *how* they do these things. According to the French historian Fernand Braudel, fashion affects everything. "It covers ideas as much as costume, the current phrase as much as the coquettish gesture, the manner of receiving at table, the care taken in sealing a letter."[2] There is no reason to think that architecture is immune.

If style is the language of architecture, fashion represents the wide—and swirling—cultural currents that shape and direct that language. Gothic architecture originated in France in the twelfth century, and remained in fashion in Europe for the next three hundred years. It was used in the great cathedrals, and in such secular masterpieces as the Doge's Palace in Venice, and the Westminster Hall in London. One of the last great Italian Gothic buildings was Milan Cathedral, begun in 1385. It was so large that the domical vault and crossing were not built until 55 years later by the great architect Filippo Brunelleschi. By then the

Renaissance was well under way, thanks to Brunelleschi's Foundling Hospital in Florence, generally considered the first building designed in the revived Classical style. With the rediscovery of Greek and Roman Classicism, Gothic became distinctly unfashionable. The old monuments were preserved, but they were not admired. "A fantastical and licentious manner of building," is how Christopher Wren characterized Gothic architecture. So general was the dissatisfaction, that *Gothic* came to stand for anything that was considered wild, barbarous, or crude.

In the mid-eighteenth century, the term Gothic reappeared, not in architecture but in literature. The Gothic romance, a type of novel, was usually set in the medieval past and involved the fantastic and the supernatural. Jane Austen's heroine in *Northanger Abbey* is a devotee of such books and spends many hours in "the luxury of a raised, restless, and frightened imagination over the pages of Udolpho." Austen is referring to Anne Radcliffe's *The Mysteries of Udolpho,* one of the most popular Gothic romances of the day, whose setting is a mysterious castle in the Apennines. Such surroundings—monasteries, dungeons, castles—figured prominently in Gothic tales ever since Horace Walpole's *The Castle of Otranto,* which was published in 1764 and is generally considered the first Gothic romance.

In her novel Austen pokes fun at the genre. The abbey of

the title is not a haunted ruin in Italy but a converted medieval building in Gloucestershire, complete with modern fireplaces, comfortable furniture, and other domestic conveniences. This is a reminder that by 1798, when *Northanger Abbey* was written, the Gothic fashion had embraced architecture. Horace Walpole was responsible for that fashion, too. In the 1750s, he had begun a project to enlarge Strawberry Hill, his Thames-side villa near London. While his contemporaries built stately houses in a delicate Classical style that was popularized by Robert and James Adam, the young Walpole, who had an independent frame of mind, looked elsewhere for inspiration. He had been an undergraduate at King's College, Cambridge and admired its extraordinary Gothic chapel. The exterior of his house was battlemented like a medieval castle. The interior combined historicism with a playful eclecticism. Motifs copied from medieval altar screens ornamented the rooms—stained glass was used in windows and papier-mâché fan-vaults covered the ceiling. Walpole's extensive collection of historical and modern books, paintings, and curiosities was also mixed in.

Walpole, the Fourth Earl of Orford, spent his entire life enlarging his house. He eventually added a cloister, a gallery, and a tower. As he was an author and a public figure who corresponded with a wide circle of literary and

Fig. 17 (RIGHT). The Holbein Room at Horace Walpole's Strawberry Hill residence, an early example of the revival of Gothic architecture in the late eighteenth century.

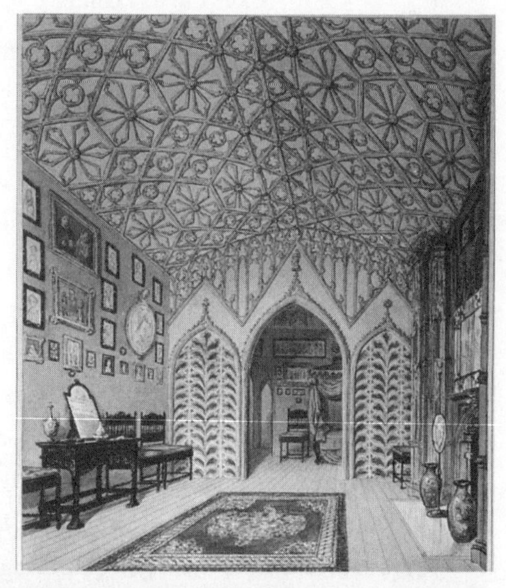

Fig. 18 (BELOW). The Gothic style also was chosen for the Canadian Houses of Parliament.

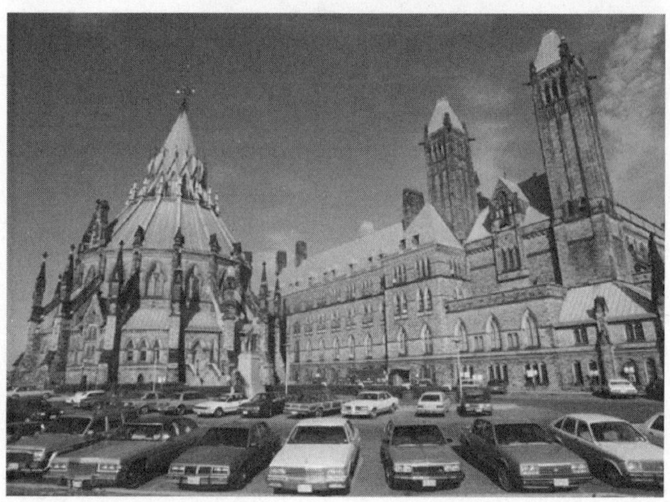

artistic friends throughout Europe, the Gothic design of Strawberry Hill became famous among connoisseurs. (It also became a tourist attraction, much to Walpole's chagrin.) Architects and their clients now saw medieval buildings as sources of inspiration, just as they had once looked to ancient Greece and Rome. The Gothic style became an established alternative for building country houses, and pointed arches appeared in décor and furniture. Gothic was "in" again.

The revived interest in the Middle Ages was complicated, for fashion is rarely one-dimensional. *Gothic* meant different things to different people (sometimes different things to the same people). Spooky Gothic novels appealed to readers. Medieval buildings appealed to the current taste for the romantic and the picturesque. Goethe's 1772 essay on Strassburg Cathedral pointed the way; he admitted to being "a sworn enemy of the tangled arbitrariness of Gothick ornament," but found himself overcome by the grandeur and mystery of the building, which he described as "a most sublime, wide-arching Tree of God." The French architectural theorist Eugène Viollet-le-Duc, on the other hand, was attracted by what he interpreted as the rationalism of Gothic construction. So was his English counterpart, George Gilbert Scott, who considered Gothic more "modern" than Classical architecture, hence a more appropriate model for architects. Augustus Welby Pugin, who worked on the British Houses of Parliament, saw a moral dimension to Gothic. He considered medieval architecture to be the ideal of Christian civilization, much as Greece and Rome had been admired as the cradle of classical—but pagan—civilization. John Ruskin, too, considered Gothic a moral force, but since he also loved Venice, polychrome Ruskinian Gothic has many Italian overtones. This incongruity is particularly striking since in England especially (but also in France and Germany), the Gothic style was considered a homegrown product—as opposed to Mediterranean Classicism. This was another cultural appeal of Gothic: at a time of growing nationalism in northern Europe, it conveniently provided a "national" style.

In North America, Gothic was, if anything, even more popular. Canadians chose a British architect and the Gothic style for their Houses of Parliament, which stand on a dramatic bluff overlooking the Ottawa River. Anglophile Americans built Collegiate Gothic campuses, Gothic parish churches, and a Gothic National Cathedral in Washington, D.C. Ralph Adams Cram, who was devoted to High Gothic, built the nave and west front of New York City's Cathedral Church of St. John the Divine, the largest Gothic structure in the world. Cram's partner Bertram Goodhue used a looser Gothic style in the military academy at West Point, as did Cass Gilbert in the Woolworth Building—the so-called Cathedral of Commerce. By then the cultural attributes of Gothic had worn thin. Hood's Chicago Tribune Building, completed in 1924, was one of the last prominent buildings designed in the Gothic style.

Gothic has not—so far—come back into fashion. Early in his career, Paul Rudolph designed a building for Wellesley College that attempted to relate architecturally to the Collegiate Gothic surroundings. It was his first large commission, and it was not a success. "Wellesley shook me," Rudolph later recalled, "and I returned to the International Style in my next building."[3] Eero Saarinen built a Gothicized dormitory at Vasser. Philip Johnson and John Burgee designed a Gothic-inspired skyscraper in Pittsburgh that was a giant abstracted glass version of the British Houses of Parliament. This was one of several stylistic forays that Johnson and Burgee made in the 1980s, including a Chippendale-top skyscraper in New York, a French Provincial high-rise in Dallas, and a neo-Burnhamesque tower in Chicago. None is particularly satisfactory, perhaps because they lack conviction. Moshe Safdie's National Gallery of Canada in Ottawa is more successful. It mimics the Gothic chapter house-cum-library of the adjacent parliament buildings in a crystalline structure of steel and glass. This episode in Safdie's oeuvre was unique, however, and Gothicized forms do not reappear in his later buildings.

The Classical style has proved more durable. This has something to do with its remarkable adaptability. Whether building an administrative center for the British Raj or designing a station for the Pennsylvania Railroad workable solutions can be devised in the Classical tradition. The cultural overtones of the Classical style are even richer than those of Gothic; they include not only the ancient civilizations of Greece and Rome, but also Renaissance Italian humanism, seventeenth-century Parisian splendor, Georgian London elegance, and English country-house comfort. During the immediate postwar period monumental Classical buildings also acquired authoritarian associations, since they had been fashionable in Nazi Germany and Stalinist Soviet Union. If Gothic was considered a national style by some English architects in the 1800s, Classicism, rooted in the early days of the Republic, has a claim to being America's national style. This is most evident in Washington, D.C. Except for brief flirtations with Victorian Gothic (the Smithsonian) and functionalist modernism (the Air and Space Museum), Classicism has remained in fashion for federal buildings ever since the construction of the Palladian White House. Washingtonian Classicism has taken many guises, ranging from the Jefferson Memorial (a small version of the Pantheon), to the severely abstract Federal Reserve Board Building. The Federal Triangle and the recent Ronald W. Reagan Building are modern interpretations of the Classical tradition.

While the architecture of federal Washington sometimes overwhelms foreign visitors, it is comfortably familiar to most Americans because of the popularity of a simplified version of Classicism—the so-called American Colonial style, which could more accurately be called American Georgian. In furnishings, décor, and above all in house design, this has been the dominant domestic fashion for the last hundred years. The origin of American Colonial can be dated with some accuracy. January 1874 was the inaugural issue of *The New York Sketchbook of Architecture.* It was edited by a youthful Charles McKim. The purpose of the publication, McKim wrote, was to document in sketches and photographs, "the beautiful, quaint, and picturesque features which belong to so many buildings, now almost disregarded, of our Colonial and Revolutionary Period." McKim and his new partners, William Mead and Stanford White, made several sketching trips in New England. They were designers, not preservationists, and their interest was the inspiration found in old buildings. White clapboard walls, black shutters, and pedimented porches started to appear in McKim, Mead & White houses. The 1876 Centen-

Fig. 19. A house in Levittown, New York, where the Cape Cod cottage style was mass produced.

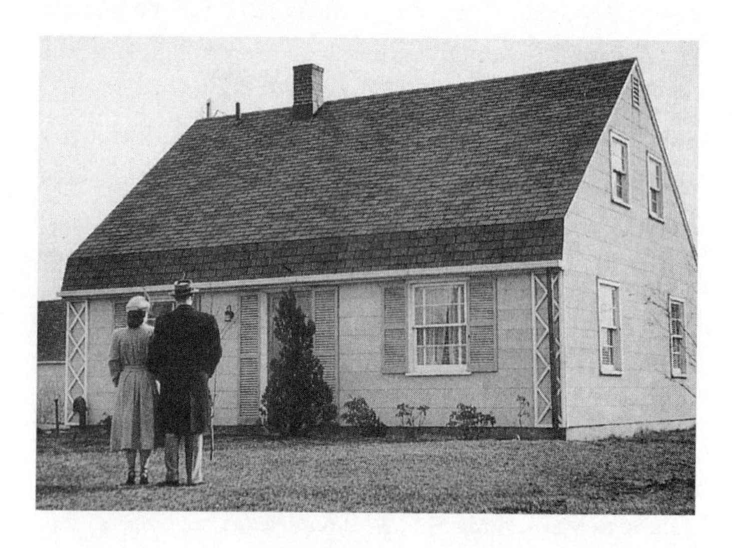

nial celebrations made the American public aware of its ancestral past. On a practical level, the understated, comfortable Colonial style was well-suited to prevailing domestic taste. It was also easily—and inexpensively—adapted to small houses. American Colonial remained the height of fashion until the 1940s. In a simplified form—the Cape Cod cottage—it reappeared in postwar Levittowns. It continues today, although the clapboard siding may be vinyl, the columns polystyrene, and the stamped metal shutters more likely symbolic than real.

"The Tribune and Radiator Buildings are both in the 'vertical' style or what is called 'Gothic' simply because I happened to make them so," Raymond Hood once flippantly explained. "If at the time of designing them I had been under the spell of Italian campaniles or Chinese pagodas, I suppose the resulting compositions would have been 'horizontal.' "[4] Hood was no more comfortable discussing style than other architects. He left unexplained the question of what had put him "under the spell" of Gothic in the first place. It had happened early: Hood's senior thesis at M.I.T.—he later also studied at the Ecole—had been a church in the Gothic style; his first employer was the Gothicist Ralph Adams Cram; and Hood assisted Bertram Goodhue on West Point. Later in life, Hood occasionally returned to the Gothic style, notably in the handsome Masonic Temple and Scottish Rite Cathedral in Scranton, Pennsylvania, but he never explained what broke the spell and led him to a more abstract style.

Like any successful architect, Hood had a strong sense of his changing time. It is easy to misunderstand the nature of that change. The abstraction that characterizes the Daily News Building and the RCA Building has little to do with new technology or changing functions. Those buildings are not any more "modern" than the Chicago Tribune tower, which had gargoyles and flying buttresses but was an advanced building in terms of planning and technology. Indeed, Hood's Gothic design was more functionally advanced than Eliel Saarinen's stylistically progressive second-place entry. It was not commodity and firmness that drove the changing aesthetic, but fashion. The public had a taste for simpler, forward-looking design, of which the International Style was but one expression. Art Deco, streamlined modern, and stripped Classicism were evidence of the same changing taste. Many industrial products of the 1930s displayed the same chic simplicity: Raymond Loewy's curvilinear Coldspot refrigerator, Walter Dorwin Teague's popular Kodak Brownie camera, Henry Dreyfuss' Bell telephone, Loewy's redesigned Coca-Cola bottle and the sleek Zippo cigarette lighter.

The medieval inventors of the Gothic style were likewise influenced by fashion. In the twelfth century, European cathedral builders abandoned the tried-and-true round arch in favor of the pointed arch. This change cannot be explained by functional or structural requirements, since the pointed arch provides only marginal structural advantages; and round-arch technology is perfectly capable of building tall naves, as Durham Cathedral and other magnificent Romanesque churches demonstrate. Cathedral builders obviously found something delightful in the pointed arch, which they used not only as a structural form, but in window tracery, in wood paneling, and even in choir-stall furniture and liturgical accessories. "[Gothic] was seized upon as essential not because it was materially essential, but because the pointed arch struck that note of fantasy which was what the mind of the age desired," explains John Summerson. "It willfully destroyed the discipline of the round arch, which had become an incubus and a bore."[5] A note of fantasy? A bore? At this point, the eminent architectural historian sounds like *a Harper's Bazaar* fashion critic.

Architectural reputations, as well as architecture, come under fashion's sway. Hood, Ely Jacques Kahn, and Ralph Walker (the architect of the Irving Trust Building on Wall Street), all small men, were dubbed the "Three Little

Napoleons of Architecture" by *The New Yorker*. Riding high in the 1920s, their careers were cut short by the Depression—Hood's more so, since he died in 1934, only 53 years old. Rockefeller Center continued to be admired by the public, but because of his freewheeling approach to design, Hood was marginalized by modernist architectural historians. He was never forgiven for winning the Chicago Tribune competition and beating not only Saarinen, but such European avant-gardists as Adolf Loos, Bruno Taut, and even Walter Gropius, the founder of the Bauhaus and the guiding light of the International Style. Yet if I compare Hood's RCA Building with Gropius's Pan Am (today MetLife) Building, there is little doubt who was the more creative designer.

Looking at that monolith, bestriding Park Avenue without charm or grace, it is easy to forget that Gropius was once considered one of the great architects of the twentieth century. Architectural memory can be fickle. Thomas Ustick Walter is not a household name, but it should be—he was the architect of the U.S. Capitol dome, probably one of the most powerful symbols of American democracy. The Lincoln Memorial, designed by Henry Bacon, is another famous architectural icon. Bacon died in 1924, only two years after the memorial was dedicated, so he did not see the Classicism that he had learned at McKim's knee slip out of fashion. At least Walter and Bacon were feted during their lifetimes. Edward Durrell Stone, an International Style *wunderkind*, developed an unfashionable interest in decoration at a time when architectural austerity was in vogue. And although he received large commissions (including the Kennedy Center for the Arts), he finished his career ignored if not actually ridiculed. In the mid-1960s, Paul Rudolph was probably the most promising young architect in the country. His robustly monumental Art and Architecture Building at Yale, where he was also chairman, reinvigorated postwar American architecture. A decade later, heroic monumentalism was out and Postmodernism was in. Although Rudolph continued to receive commissions in Asia, he was slighted in his own country. His contemporaries Gordon Bunshaft and Kevin Roche were awarded the Pritzker Prize, but Rudolph was passed over. By the time he died in 1997, he was virtually forgotten.

Yet Rudolph, a gifted designer, may be admitted to the architectural pantheon one day. Architectural reputations can rise and fall and rise again. The nineteenth-century Philadelphia architect Frank Furness designed Ruskinian Gothic buildings whose lively eclecticism anticipates James Stirling. Furness, an exceptional individual who won a Congressional Medal of Honor during the Civil War, dominated the Philadelphia architectural scene for 20 years. In 1891 he

Fig. 20. Frank Furness's University of Pennsylvania library, once slated for demolition, has become the best-loved building on campus.

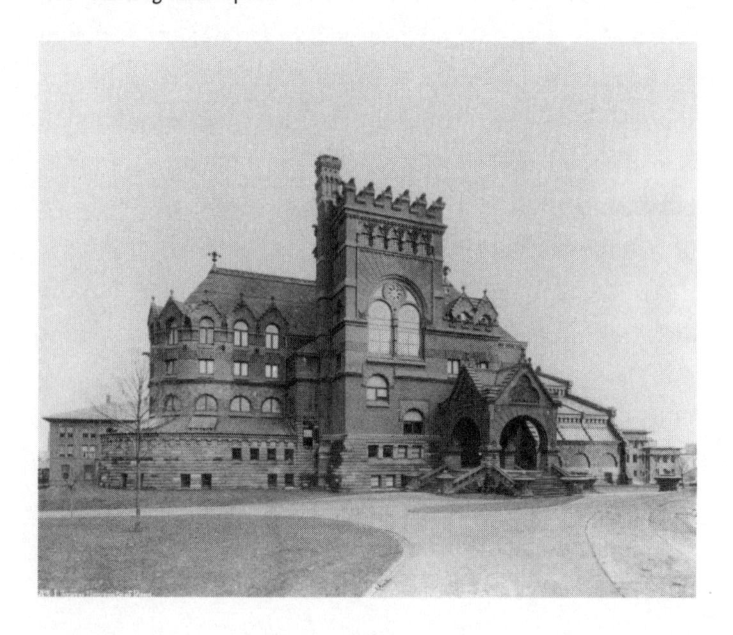

completed the University of Pennsylvania Library, a widely acclaimed brick and terracotta building with a dramatic four-story-high reading room. After the turn-of-the-century, with Classicism all the rage, Furness' idiosyncratic brand of architecture became unfashionable. Although he lived until 1912, his practice languished. In time he was entirely forgotten, many of his buildings were demolished, others insensitively altered. As for the library, its tall reading room was crudely truncated by a suspended ceiling. In the 1950s, there was a revival of interest in Furness, which narrowly saved the library from demolition. Today, after a careful restoration, the library is unquestionably the best-loved building on the University of Pennsylvania campus—something about the spiky decoration and the willfully manipulated forms appeals to current sensibility. Furness has found an audience again.

The fate of Rudolph and Furness is a reminder that although architecture is susceptible to fashion, architects are not fashion designers. "I do not design a new architecture every Monday morning," Mies van der Rohe is reputed to have said. This is often taken as a reflection of his serious commitment to his art. It was that, but it was something else, too. He might as well have said, "*I cannot* design a new architecture every Monday morning." The Seagram Building is a masterpiece, not because Mies had a sudden inspiration, but because he had spent decades learning how to bring commodity, firmness, and delight into his particular version of balance; how to attach the travertine to the wall to create a particular effect; which metal fabricator could make a certain kind of handrail; and exactly how deep to make a window mullion to cast the right size of shadow. Buildings are extremely complicated artifacts, and the time necessary to cultivate and refine a particular manner of building cannot be underestimated. This is especially true when the manner of building is personal or unusual, as it was in the case of both Furness and Rudolph. They were not simply being stubborn or high-minded when they refused to adapt to changing fashions, they were being realistic.

Morris Lapidus is an architect who has lived long enough to see architectural fashions come full circle. In the 1950s, Lapidus designed many of the largest hotels in the Miami area: the Fontainebleau, the Americana, the Eden Roc. His flamboyant, eclectic designs were ridiculed by the architectural establishment, although they were popular with the public. Today, in a period of so-called entertainment architecture, when the world's most celebrated architects design theme parks and casinos, Lapidus seems less like a maverick than a pioneer. "The father of us all," Philip Johnson called him, with only slight exaggeration.

• • •

Architecture changes at a bewildering pace. Consider only the last 50 years of museum design. The National Gallery of Art (1937-41) in Washington, D.C. and the Museum of Modern Art (1937-39) in New York City are almost exact contemporaries. In the MoMA design, Philip L. Goodwin and Edward Durrell Stone ignored the Classical tradition represented by John Russell Pope's masterpiece. MoMA's entrance was not up a broad flight of exterior steps but through a revolving door. Goodwin and Stone replaced the monumental rotunda by a nondescript lobby, the lofty galleries by low-ceilinged loft spaces, and limestone and marble by stucco and plasterboard. MoMA was to be the last word in avant-garde International Style, but it was scarcely finished when it was challenged by Frank Lloyd Wright's Guggenheim Museum (1943-58), which rejected the banality of the white box by squeezing the entire museum into a dramatic sculptural spiral. Nothing could be further from the International Style than the mollusk-like exterior (especially if it had been tinted rose-red, as Wright initially wanted). In the Yale Center for British Art (1969-77), Louis I. Kahn likewise incorporated central skylit spaces, but he disavowed Wright's loud anti-urban exterior by hugging the sidewalk and clothing his building in drab stainless steel panels. Kahn preached taming technology by consigning it to so-called servant spaces; in the Centre Georges Pompidou (1971-77), Piano and Rogers stood Kahn's dictum on its head and gave the servants the run of the house. In the Neue Staatsgalerie (1977-83), James Stirling cheekily lifted architectural elements from both the Pompidou and the Guggenheim and combined them with a variety of historical styles. I. M. Pei's impeccably crafted East Building of the National Gallery of Art (1976-78) in Washington, D.C., had not one exposed bolt, not one allusion to the past. Pei rejected both Stirling's eclecticism and Piano and Rogers' technological posturing. Instead he relied on abstract geometry for architectural effect. Frank O. Gehry's California Aerospace Museum (1982-84) in Los Angeles is no less abstract and geometrical, but his forms bump and grind into each other almost as if by accident. "I really enjoy the awkwardness with which [the forms] touch," Gehry observed, "as it reminds me of the cities we live in and the kind of awkwardnesses of city buildings sitting next to each other."[6] The cost of the East Building was $94.4 million; the Aerospace Museum was built on a tight budget of only $3.4 million. Lacking money for refinement, Gehry turned awkwardness into a virtue, and in the process disowned Pei's fastidious brand of modernism. He was carefree where Pei was careful, spontaneous where Pei was studied, brash where Pei was genteel. The Aerospace Museum was clearly not a cheaper version of the East Building, it was something different.

"Fashion is also a search for a new language to discredit the old," writes Fernand Braudel, "a way in which each generation can repudiate its immediate predecessor and distinguish itself from it."[7] This puts fashion in the right light: it may be fleeting, but it is not frivolous. As Braudel suggests, changes in fashion imply not only the creation of something new, but the destruction of something old. That is why new fashions are inevitably upsetting. Whether one is wearing a lounge-suit instead of a frock coat, or turning a baseball cap backwards, someone else is bound to be insulted. No less so in architecture. Replacing an Ionic column with a steel I-beam, or exposing air-conditioning ducts, or using common materials in uncommon ways are calculated affronts to honored conventions. "We are not like our fathers," the architects say, "we are different."

THREE
STYLE

When an architectural competition was announced for the New York Public Library on May 21, 1897, Dr. John Shaw Billings, the library's executive director, was determined that in his building, design would not triumph over function. He had in mind Boston's newly built public library, a beautiful but in his opinion poorly functioning building. Billings, an ex-army physician, was responsible for organizing the Surgeon General's Library and a celebrated medical index. He was also an expert in hospital design, and was thus familiar with building construction. He drafted a plan for the new library whose most unorthodox feature was the location of the main reading room. It was not located near the main entrance, as was common practice, but on an upper floor, above the book stacks.

The terms of the architectural competition were strict

Fig. 21. Carrère & Hastings' New York Public Library, built from a design that beat established firms.

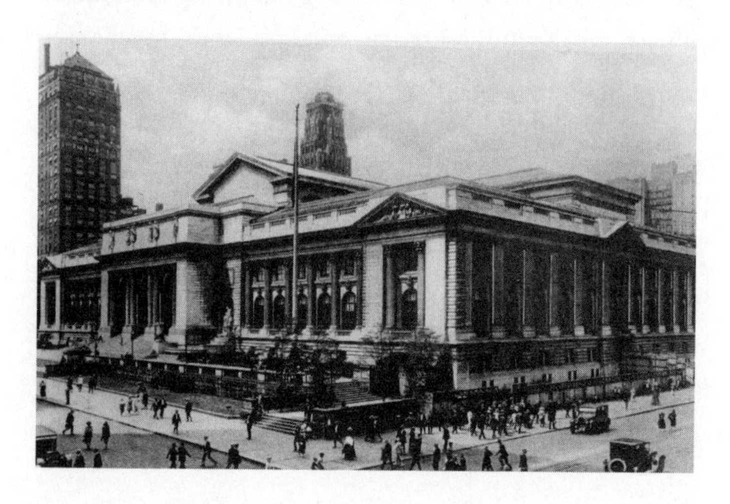

and included detailed floor plans that the competitors were required to follow. There were two stages, intended to attract new talent as well as established firms. First, six architects were chosen from an open competition. These six then advanced to a second stage, where they competed against six invited firms that included not only McKim, Mead & White (the architects of the Boston Public Library), but also such luminaries as Peabody & Stearns, George B. Post, and an up-and-coming young firm, Carrère & Hastings. The up-and-comers carried the day. McKim, much to his chagrin, not only lost but placed third behind Howard & Cauldwell. It was his own fault, since he imperiously ignored the suggested plan and substituted his own arrangement. Carrère & Hastings conscientiously followed Billings' requirements.

The projected budget for the new library was not large ($1.7 million) and Billings expected a relatively modest building.* That was not what he got. All three designs were monumental. Carrère & Hastings and Howard & Cauldwell used the Modern French style, which was more ornate and allowed for more articulation to the façade than the austere Classical style that McKim opted for. All incorporated giant columns rising the full height of the two floors—

*The budget was later expanded and the final cost of the library was $9 million.

Corinthian in McKim's case, Ionic in the other two (the completed building is Corinthian). The compositional strategies were roughly similar: a monumental stair led to an elevated main floor; the entrance was placed in the center (more understated in McKim's elegant design); statuary and urns adorned the attic. All three entrants shared a sense of what was beautiful and what was appropriate, and all were concerned with conveying the same message of permanence, dignity, and of culture rooted in the past.

I mentioned the New York Public Library competition when I gave a public lecture in connection with a recent architectural competition for the new Salt Lake City Public Library. The library board had conducted a national search for an architect, visited new libraries across the country, and solicited proposals from prominent architects. They had narrowed their list to four firms: Charles Gwathmey and Robert Siegel are respected New York architects with a long record of university buildings and museums, including a new library of science, industry, and business for the New York Public Library system. Moshe Safdie had built major civic buildings in Israel, Canada, and the United States, and recently completed the public library in Vancouver, British Columbia. Moore Ruble Yudell is a Los Angeles firm founded by the late Charles Moore, with whom John Ruble and Buzz Yudell built several university libraries and a public library in Berlin. Will Bruder, the least well-known of the four, is a southwesterner and the architect of the new, well-regarded Phoenix Public Library.

I told my audience that I thought that the Salt Lake City library board would have a more difficult choice than their nineteenth-century New York counterparts. It was not a question of function. The Salt Lake City librarians had prepared an equally exhaustive program of requirements, so whichever architect was chosen *commodity* probably would be well served. As for *firmness,* I was reasonably sure that any of these experienced firms would build soundly. It was the consideration of *delight* that would make the selection harder. Gwathmey and Siegel design crisply detailed, understated buildings in a latter-day version of the International Style. Safdie, too, is a modernist, but he follows in the footsteps of Pei, and his buildings are frankly monumental—the Vancouver library had been likened to the Roman Coliseum. Moore Ruble Yudell's work is different. Informal and animated, their eclectic Postmodern designs are likely to include ornament and architectural motifs drawn from their surroundings. Bruder, on the other hand, designs chic buildings that incorporate exposed structural elements, rough industrial materials, and sleek details. Building on the same site, fulfilling the same functional requirements, and using the same up-to-date construction technology, the four firms would produce libraries that would *look* different.

The library board awarded the commission to Moshe Safdie, and a year later the plans for the new building were unveiled. The new library will feature an unusual triangular-shaped main building and a curving wall-like structure that encloses a public square. A hundred years ago, it was taken for granted that the New York Public Library would be designed in some variant of the Classical style. Today a public library can take many guises. It can be relentlessly avant-garde, like the new $1.5 billion national library in Paris, where the books are housed in four L-shaped 22-story glass towers, and the readers are lodged in underground rooms, which the London *Times* described as "a series of rectangular salons (identical of course) where you can admire the ultra-smooth gray concrete, steel grille ceilings and the expanses of African veneer."[1] A new library can be comfortably Modernist, like the new British Library in London, which the *Independent* humorously described as "a giant municipal building that has made its way from Scandinavia, having crashed headfirst through an English brickworks on the way."[2] Tom Beeby's handsome Harold T. Washington Library in Chicago, on the other hand, is distinctly old-fashioned, with rusticated stone walls and carved brick ornaments that are a literal evocation of the city's nineteenth-century architectural tradition. Instead of trendy plastic or metal chairs, the reading areas are equipped with solid wood tables and traditional courthouse chairs. James Ingo Freed's Main Public Library in San Francisco, on the other hand, is both old and new: the imposing granite and stainless steel exterior is more or less Classical on one façade, and more or less Modernist on another.

The coexistence of different architectural styles is nothing new. In a 1913 essay titled "Style in American Architecture," Ralph Adams Cram identified no less than seven contemporary styles, although he called them "tendencies." Five were traditional: McKim's pure Classicism; the Beaux-Arts French Modern; Colonial, which was associated with houses but was also appearing in larger buildings such as the Johns Hopkins University campus; Cram's own High Gothic; and a looser interpretation of the medieval style as practiced by his partner Goodhue. Two were new: steel-frame construction, which Cram described as an *enfant terrible*; and what he called the Secessionists—Frank Lloyd Wright in Chicago, the Greene brothers in Pasadena—who exhibited "a strongly developed enmity to archaeological forms of any kind." Cram was not sanguine about the future, but he nevertheless concluded: "Chaos then confronts us, in that there is no single architectural following, but legion; and in that fact lies the honor of our art, for neither is society one, or ever at one with itself."[3]

Cram is right: most historical periods are marked by stylistic confusion; it is stylistic consensus that is unusual.

Fig. 22. Le Corbusier's *volte face*—the pilgrimage chapel at Ronchamps.

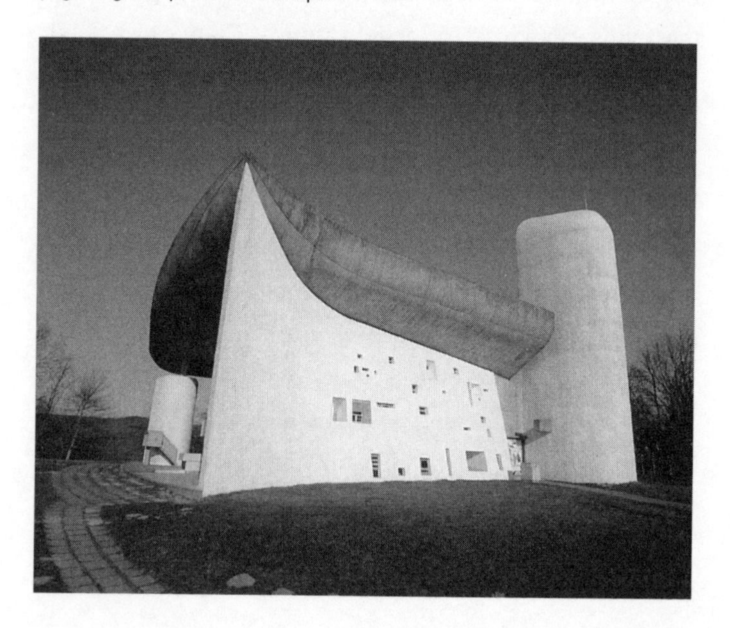

There was such a brief consensus in the late 1890s, when both architects and the American public, under the influence of the immensely popular World's Columbian Exposition, embraced Classicism, at least for public buildings. That unanimity lasted long enough for the New York Public Library competition, but it began to unravel shortly after, as Cram's essay makes clear. There was also a consensus in the 1920s, at least among progressive architects. That consensus did not last either. After 1940, Mies van der Rohe gave up the free-flowing plans and asymmetrical massing that had characterized the Barcelona Pavilion and the Tugendhat House, and began designing buildings whose details and materials were Modern but whose layout and composition were distinctly Classical. In the 1920s, Le Corbusier proclaimed the "Five Points of a New Architecture": the building raised on stilts; the roof garden; the frame structure that allowed a free plan; the free façade; and the horizontal ribbon window. He, too, had second thoughts. Thirty years later, his wonderful chapel at Ronchamps had massive sculpted wall that concealed a concrete frame; the roof, far from being flat, resembled a billowing nun's coif. Le Corbusier, who had coined the famous expression, "a house is a machine for living in," now adopted distinctly un-machinelike building materials such as crudely finished concrete, exposed brick, roughened stucco, and fieldstone.

This *volte face* gave rise to the so-called Brutalist style, which had a worldwide influence, shaping the work of architects as dissimilar as James Stirling and Paul Rudolph, and ultimately opening the door to Postmodern stylistic experiments such as Charles Moore's little house in the Berkeley hills.

The inconstancy of the International Style practitioners should have been expected. The history of Western architecture is of architects searching for rules, only to bend and break them. Even Classicism, which appears at first glance to be highly regimented, is not immune. As far as we know, the ancient Greeks used only three orders: Doric, Ionic, and Corinthian. Vitruvius describes them, and also refers to a Tuscan order, which is a Roman invention. Roman, too, is the so-called Composite order, an ornate blend of Ionic and Corinthian. The vault, the arch, and the dome, unknown to the Greeks, were other Roman additions to the Classic canon. Architects have been stretching Classical rules ever since: breaking pediments, flattening pilasters, magnifying and shrinking columns, rusticating masonry. A sixteenth-century French architect, Philibert de l'Orme, invented a French order; Edwin Lutyens devised an order based on Mughal precedents for the Viceroy's House in New Delhi; more recently, Allan Greenberg created an order for the offices of the Secretary of State that incorporated the Great

Seal of the United States. Michael Graves designed Classical caryatids (columns carved in the shape of human figures) to support the pedimented front of an office building for the Walt Disney Company in Burbank. While the supports of the porch of the Erechtheon in Athens take the form of graceful maidens, Graves' caryatids are the Seven Dwarfs.

The headquarters of a company whose logo is a pair of mouse ears obviously demands a different decorum from a temple. In the past, religious buildings and palaces required a narrow stylistic range. As architectural commissions grew to include civic and commercial buildings, warehouses, factories, shops and cinemas, houses and weekend houses—every sort of building—a single style no longer sufficed. Gothic is an evocative style for churches, but despite Walpole's efforts it is ill-adapted to houses. Romanesque makes imposing city halls, but is too heavy to be applied to skyscrapers. The International Style makes striking small buildings but monotonous large ones. Shingle Style cottages are pleasing; a Shingle Style Home Depot is ridiculous. As Cram wisely observed, "Architecture is nothing unless it is intimately expressive, and if utterly different things clamor for voicing, different also must be their architectural manifestation."[4]

The great architects—Brunelleschi, Palladio, Wren,

Richardson, Lutyens—regularly looked to the past for inspiration. In 1965, Richard Meier built the Smith House, which has been called the first International Style revival building. Like all revivalists, Meier picks and chooses. At first glance, the Smith House has all the stylistic hallmarks of a Le Corbusier villa of the 1920s: a free plan, flat roof, white walls, pipe railings, horizontal ribbon windows, a ramp. Yet it is built out of wood and steel, not masonry. The white walls are painted wood siding, not stucco; the details are more refined, the plate-glass sheets are larger, the structure lighter. The result is an International Style that is filtered through American consciousness and shaped by American technology. It is like Thomas Jefferson building Classical columns out of wood—the same, but different.

Although art historians use terms like Gothic Revival and Greek Revival to distinguish later reincarnations of styles, architects look at history differently. "For the serious architect the past exists not as a legacy to be possessed through a self-conscious act of the 'modern' will," writes Roger Scruton in *The Aesthetics of Architecture*, "but as an enduring fact, an ineliminable part of an extended present."[5] That is why architects, whether they are Inigo Jones or Louis Kahn, make architectural pilgrimages to the Mediterranean roots of Western architecture. Sketchbook in hand, they plumb the secrets of the master builders of the past. Consciousness of the past may also explain why architects tend to resist being categorized according to style; they instinctively understand that the history of architecture—including the present—is a continuity rather than a series of episodes.

Stylistic consistency is much admired today, but it was not always so. In 1419, Filippo Brunelleschi began the Foundling Hospital in Florence, whose delicate arcade of Corinthian columns surmounted by pedimented windows is generally considered the first building of the Renaissance. At the very same time, he was building a great dome over the crossing of the cathedral of Florence in a style that was not Classical but distinctly Gothic, pointed arches and all. The German architect Karl Friedrich Schinkel is best known for his severe Classical public buildings such as the superb Altes Museum in Berlin, but he also worked in other styles: Gothic in churches, and picturesque Italianate in villas. McKim, Mead & White favored the Classical style for public buildings and palatial residences, but built Norman parish churches, Shingle Style summer retreats, French Renaissance mansions, and American Colonial country houses. John Russell Pope, an eclectic master, designed beautiful picturesque Tudor, Georgian, and Colonial country estates. Edwin Lutyens was another Classicist whose residential work was eclectic.

Domestic architects had to be adaptable, because house styles changed according to fashion. In the United States, Tudor was popular in the 1900s, as was the Free Style; Cotswold and French Provincial appeared in the 1920s. After the 1930s, influenced by the restoration of Williamsburg, American Colonial returned to favor. The Cotswold style, with its relatively severe details and blunt forms, created a very different setting from French Provincial, which tended to have more delicate details, from Free Style with its almost rustic atmosphere, or from sturdy Colonial. Since historic styles carry cultural overtones, using different styles was also a way for architects—and clients—to say different things.

If architectural style is a language—an analogy that is deeply flawed—it is closer to slang than to grammatical prose. Architectural styles are mutable, unregulated, improvised. Architects break the rules, and invent new ones. In part, this is simply the irrepressible urge of creative individuals. In part, architects break stylistic rules because they *can*. After all, most of the rules that govern building design—fire codes, building codes, zoning laws, budgets, programmatic requirements, engineering norms—are outside the architect's control; stylistic rules are firmly within his purview. Since architecture is so intensely competitive, doing something unexpected, unusual, or just different is a way to be noticed, to rise above the crowd.

In addition to historical styles, there have also been styles associated with individual architects. The Palladian style made its way from Andrea Palladio to Inigo Jones, from him to Colen Campbell and Lord Burlington, and thence to Thomas Jefferson. It reappears in the work of contemporary Classicists such as Allan Greenberg. H. H. Richardson's influence was considerably shorter-lived, but for at least 20 years Richardsonian Romanesque rolled over the United States like an "aesthetic Juggernaut," in Cram's colorful phrase. Mies van der Rohe's steel-and-glass style likewise prevailed for more than two decades, and his characteristic I-beam window mullion can still be seen in contemporary curtain walls.

Buildings like Jones' Palladian Queen's House in Greenwich, Adler & Sullivan's Richardsonian Romanesque Auditorium Building in Chicago, and Gordon Bunshaft's Miesian Lever House are not copies but satisfying originals. However, most personal styles are not easily adaptable. A building in Wright's unmistakable Prairie style, for example, simply looks like a knock-off. Some personal styles are simply too obsessive, which is probably why Frank Furness and the equally idiosyncratic Barcelona architect Antonio Gaudí never attracted a following.

Inigo Jones consciously based his work on the architecture of Palladio, but he did not think of himself as working in the Palladian "style," any more than Palladio would have referred to the Classical "style." Although Renaissance architects described their architecture as *all'antica*—in the antique manner—they took it for granted that the history of architecture was a progression: the Romans improved on the Greeks, and they would improved on the Romans. According to the architecture historian Peter Collins, the use of the word *style* to designate the architecture of a particular period or country is relatively late. He cites James Stuart and Nicholas Revett's *Antiquities of Athens,* published in 1762 and credited with inaugurating the Classical Revival in England. The authors, both architects, referred to "the Grecian and Roman style of building."[6]

The Latin root of "style" is *stilus.* A *stilus* was the sharp-pointed tool used to write on wax tablets and, by inference, *stilus* also referred to the way that something was written. This sense of technique carried over to English, and the original meaning of *style* was those features of literary composition that belonged to the form rather than to the substance of the matter being expressed. The seventeenth-century English musical composer Samuel Wesley put it neatly: "Style is the dress of thought." Jacques-François Blondel, who was Louis XV's architect and who founded the first full-time school of architecture in Europe in 1750, adopted this literary meaning as a metaphor and described architectural style as a building's character—for example, rustic, regal, or heroic. "Style in the organization of façades and in the decoration of rooms is the poetry of architecture," he taught his students, "which alone makes all the architect's compositions truly interesting."[7]

Literary style described the way that something was written, expressed, or performed. Architectural style, in Blondel's sense, describes the way that something was built. Although architecture is often defined in terms of abstractions such as space, light, and volume, buildings are above all physical artifacts. The experience of architecture is palpable: the grain of wood, the veined surface of marble, the cold precision of steel, the textured pattern of brick. But exactly what do we see when we look at brickwork? We see the joints between the bricks and the mortar (which can be flush, or scraped out to create shadows; the bonding patterns; the way that the bricks turn the corner; the surrounding of openings; and the connection between the brick wall and the foundation or the eaves. What we see are details.

Details are a major preoccupation of the architect. Once the overall form of a building is determined—"the masterly, correct, and magnificent play of masses brought together in light"—there remains the question not only of what materials are to be used and how these will be assembled, but also of how the hundreds of parts of the building are to be designed: from the door frames and the window sills to the railings and the baseboards.

The function of a baseboard is to cover the joint between the wall and the floor, and secondarily to protect the wall from scuffing. There are dozens of ways that this can be done. Baseboards can be prominent or discreet, a complicated assembly of board, cap and base, or a simple strip of hardwood. Or nothing—many modern architects dispense with baseboards altogether. The baseboards in my living room are twelve inches tall. They are not wood but cast iron, since they are really disguised radiators. My house was built in 1908, influenced by the British Free Style of Voysey and Baillie Scott, and to further preserve a simple, rustic atmosphere the architect had the baseboards/radiators painted to resemble wood.

Railings have a simple function—they must be sturdy enough to support us if we lean on them, and they must provide a secure hand-hold: if railings are open, the spaces between the supports and the rails should be small enough to prevent children from falling through. Classical railings, developed during the Renaissance, consist of balusters supporting a handrail. Balusters—little columns—can have a single or a double swelling curve, or a vase shape. Fabricated in wood or masonry, they can be round or square in cross-section, and plain or highly ornamented. Railings can be replaced by parapets with pierced screens. These can be stone or metal: bronze, wrought, or cast iron. The screens can be simple X-shapes, intertwining geometrical patterns, or complicated floral figures as in Art Nouveau staircases. Perhaps the simplest open railings are those of the great Adirondack camps, whose builders mimicked X-shaped wrought-iron railings in unpeeled rustic tree trunks.

Modern railings are usually metal. In his early villas, Le Corbusier used white-painted pipe railings to create a nautical image; in later buildings like the Carpenter Center for the Visual Arts at Harvard, flat steel bars take the place of pipes. The railings in Mies van der Rohe's buildings usually have only a single intermediate rail, located precisely halfway between the handrail and the floor; the vertical stanchions, the handrail, and the rail are made of identical square steel bars. The railings in Louis Kahn buildings tend to be parapets, but where he is obliged to use an open railing the design is as simple as possible. I have seen a short stair railing that consisted of a single bronze bar, bent at each end to form the uprights. Richard Meier uses metal railings, too, but because there are sometimes as many as six horizontal rails, the visual effect is more pronounced—they resemble staffs in sheet music.

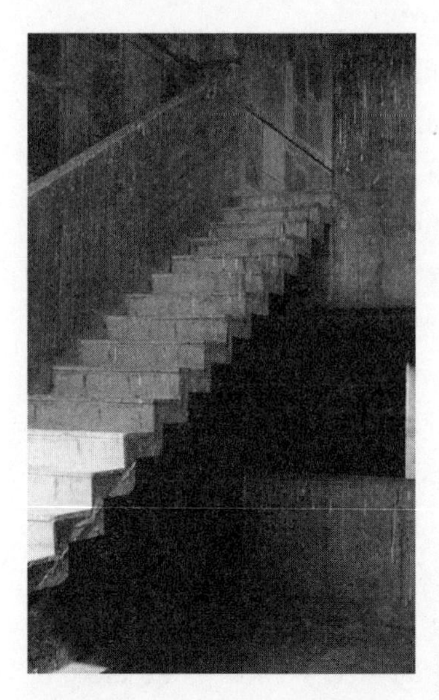

Fig. 23 (BELOW, LEFT). Steel cables are used instead of railings in Bernard Tschumi's Lerner Center at Columbia University.

Fig. 24 (BELOW, RIGHT). Tempered glass allows the railings in I.M. Pei's East Building in the National Gallery of Art appear to hover above the floor.

Fig. 25 (LEFT). No railing at all in Le Corbusier's proto-Brutalist Shodhan house in Ahmedabad, India, 1956.

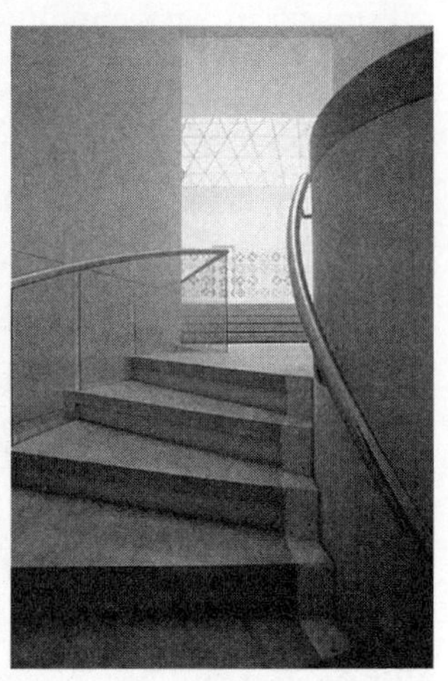

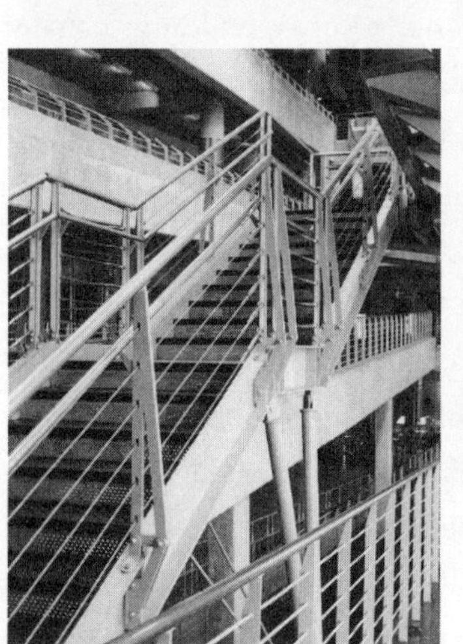

When Brutalism was in fashion, railings were correspondingly heavy: concrete beams, wide enough to sit on but unpleasant to the touch, or massive wood balustrades, as solid as fenders on a truck dock. The vogue among many younger architects today is toward lightness and exposed construction, and railings reflect that fashion, too. The screens of the railings of Peter Rose's Canadian Center for Architecture in Montreal are industrial-looking perforated sheets of anodized aluminum, prominently bolted to the stanchions. Bernard Tschumi substitutes steel cables (complete with turnbuckles) for the intermediate horizontal rails of the ramp railings of Lerner Hall at Columbia University, another nautical reference, but to a yacht rather than a steamship. These solutions appear mannered compared to the simple railing that I. M. Pei designed for the East Building of the National Gallery. The stainless steel handrail highlights the solidity of the rose-colored Tennessee marble by appearing to float in mid-air, since it is supported by continuous sheets of tempered glass embedded in the floor.

The transparent railings of I. M. Pei's East Building are understated, elegant, and luxurious—like the building. "Beauty will result from the form and correspondence of the whole with respect to the several parts," taught Palladio, "of the parts with regard to each other, and of these again to the whole."[8] The successful relationship of the details to each other, and to the building is governed by the architect's sense of style. That is why the architect of my house painted the radiators to resemble wood; a technologically inclined architect might have painted them silver; a minimalist would dispense with baseboards and hide the radiators in the wall. The role of details is not to complement architecture; details *are* architecture. "The aesthetic understanding [of architecture]," writes Roger Scruton, "is inseparable from a sense of detail."[9] Mies van der Rohe is supposed to have said "God is in the details."* He did not mean that details are functionally important (although they are), or that good details prolong the life of a building (although they do). He meant that details are the soul of architecture. That is why, just as an archaeologist can reconstruct a pot from a few shards, or a paleontologist can surmise the form of a prehistoric animal from bone fragments, it is possible to divine the architect's idea of a building by examining its details.

The house that Robert Venturi built for his mother in 1964 shook the foundations of the International Style; much of this effect was the result of details. Although Venturi obviously was working in a Modernist idiom—there is

*Like Mies' famous "less is more," the origin of this statement is obscure. "God is in the details" is variously attributed to Mies, to art historian Aby Warburg, to Gustave Flaubert, and to Saint Teresa of Avila.

a strip window and a steel-pipe railing—he also incorporated distinctly un-Modernist features such as trim, both inside and out. Classical architects use a large variety of moldings—fillet, astragal, egg and dart, ogee—that can be combined and recombined to great decorative effect. The International Style, in its effort to do away with ornament, outlawed trim. Walls were flat planes. Windows had no frames. Joints between materials were simply hairline cracks. The conspicuous exterior dado, the baseboards, and the chair-rails in the Vanna Venturi House were hardly Classical moldings—they were merely boards with chamfered edges—yet they challenged the assumption that trim and Modernism were incompatible.

Coming through the front door of the Vanna Venturi House one immediately senses that it is an unusual place. A broad stair rises beside the fireplace, then peters out to almost nothing. The fireplace looks like an abstract sculpture, but it has a traditional mantelpiece. A free-standing column à la Corbusier stands beside a chair-rail. Then there is the furniture. Ever since the Tugendhat House—for which Mies had designed the furniture—it was taken for granted that modern houses required modern furniture. Venturi has explained that "I designed the house so my mother's old furniture (c. 1925, plus some antiques) would look good in it."[10] Instead of the iconic bent-tube Breuer

Fig. 26. The interior of the Vanna Venturi house, designed by Robert Venturi for his mother.

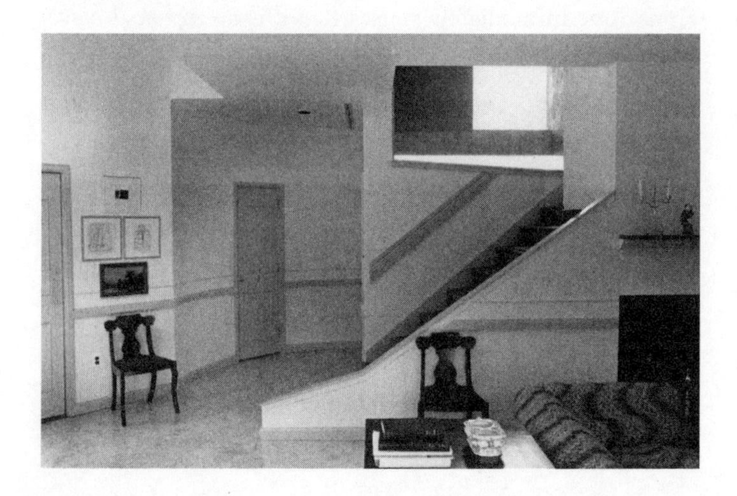

chairs, there are homely ladderback chairs around the dining table; instead of an Eames lounge chair and ottoman, a comfortable stuffed sofa. It is a contradictory atmosphere—the International Style willfully distorted through the lens of traditional bourgeois domesticity.

Whether one is looking up at the tall dome of the Pantheon, descending the spiraling vortex of Wright's Guggenheim Museum, or standing in the living room of Venturi's small house, the experience of architecture is above all the experience of being in a separate, distinct world. That is what distinguishes architecture from sculpture—it is not an object but a place. The sense of being in a special place that is a three-dimensional expression of the architect's imagination is one of the distinctive pleasures of architecture. To create a strong sense of place, the surroundings must be all of a piece; space, mass, shapes, and materials must reflect the same sensibility. That is why details are so important. A jarring detail or an inconsistency—something "out of place"—and the fantasy begins to crumble. Yes, fantasy. Illusion has been a part of architecture ever since the ancient Greeks made columns with a gently swelling taper to deceive the eye. This is not to say that architecture is stage décor. When the wind blows, the canvas scenery blows over; the building resists the elements. Architecture surrounds and shelters us. It is the real world but it is also a vision.

• • •

The Postmodern movement that followed the Vanna Venturi House was relatively short-lived but it had an important consequence: it broke the stranglehold of Modernism, leaving designers free to explore other forms of expression. The profusion of styles that ensued is demonstrated by the work of three gifted but vastly different architects, Allan Greenberg, Hugh Newell Jacobsen, and Enrique Norten.

Allan Greenberg is a confirmed Classicist. He does not consider this an anomaly. "To be truly modern," he writes, "means finding the dynamic balance between eternal human values and the specific demands of the present. Classical architecture provides the means to achieve this balance because it is the most comprehensive architectural language that human beings have yet developed."[11] Although Greenberg looks to the past, his is not the attitude of an archeologist. Like Carrère & Hastings, and generations of architects before them, Greenberg approaches Classicism as a tradition to be studied, absorbed—then extended.

Early in his career, after emigrating to the United States from South Africa, Greenberg was employed writing design standards for courthouses, which led to an unusual commission: the conversion of an empty supermarket into a courthouse. He gave the commercial building in Manchester, Connecticut, a new façade dominated by a large arch, over-scaled voussoirs, and a pediment. Inside, the barrel-vaulted ceiling of the lobby was supported by a Tuscan order. Greenberg had graduated from Yale in 1965, and like many of his contemporaries was experimenting with the new freedom offered by Postmodernism. However, unlike Venturi and Moore, Greenberg was not coyly introducing Classical elements into a Modernist building; he was returning to Classical roots. From this modest beginning, over the next two decades, came a variety of commissions: a suite of rooms for the Secretary of State in the United States Department of State building, several college and university buildings, and a Roman Catholic church. His commercial work included a newspaper office building in Athens, Georgia, a new entrance for Bergdorf Goodman on Fifth Avenue in Manhattan, and a flagship store for Tommy Hilfiger in Beverly Hills. Greenberg is also known for large country houses, both in the United States and in Europe. Like Lutyens and John Russell Pope, he ventures stylistically farther afield in his residential work—using Georgian and American Colonial styles. One of his early houses was inspired by Mount Vernon, another by Palladio's unfinished Villa Thiene. Several are picturesque rambling affairs whose relaxed informality recalls the best work of McKim, Mead & White.

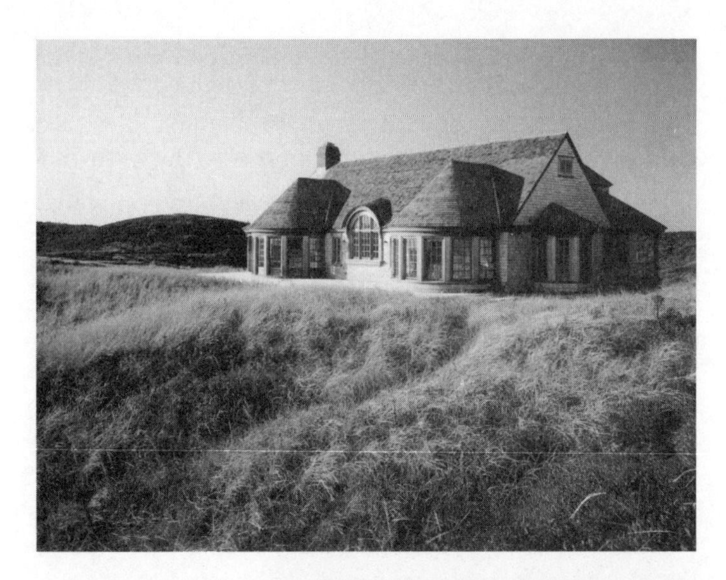

Fig. 27 (ABOVE) and Fig. 28 (RIGHT). A homey cottage on the eastern seaboard, designed by Allan Greenberg.

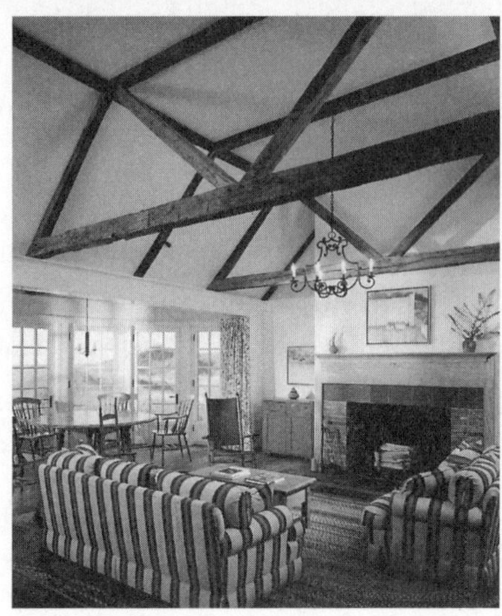

One of my favorite Greenberg houses is a cottage set among windblown dunes on the eastern seaboard. Completed in 1992, the low-lying building is shingled, but it is not exactly Shingle Style. Recent Shingle Style buildings are often broken down into many small parts, giving them a fussy and nervous appearance. Such seaside cottages look as if a good wind could blow them away. Greenberg's aim here is to make a heavyweight building of great solidity that is rooted firmly in the dune scrub. The one-story Atlantic façade is almost perfectly symmetrical: a large arched window flanked by two semi-circular bays, rotund sentinels standing against the ocean winds. The two-story landward side is more informal, ringed by a sheltered porch. Massivity informs the details: sturdy Tuscan columns, a heavy cornice at the eaves of the large roof, rugged window frames. The sense of robustness is accentuated by occasional delicacy: the arched window incorporates scrolled brackets that support an elegant reverse ogee molding at the eaves. Inside, the fireplace has a brick hearth, a slate lintel, and a wood surround, whose almost modern simplicity is softened by a cavetto molding beneath the mantelpiece. The ceiling is supported by exposed trusses of rough, reused timbers. Although most people would describe this house as "traditional," this is not an exercise in a particular historical style. There is a nod here to the British Arts and Crafts architect

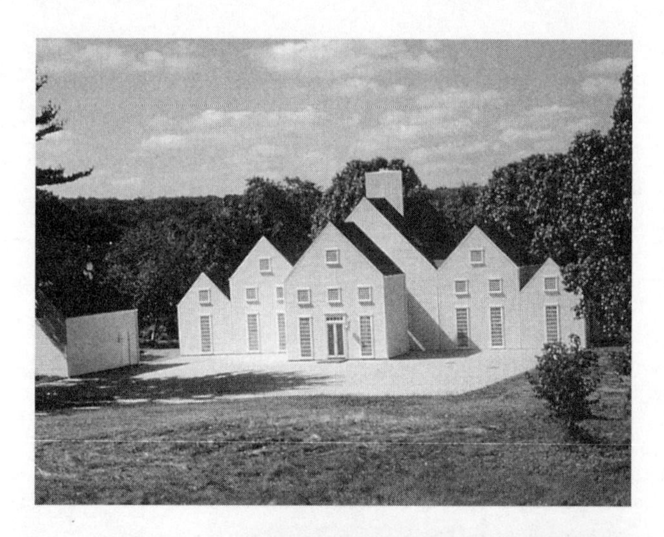

Fig. 29 (ABOVE) and Fig. 30 (RIGHT). Hugh Newell Jacobsen's stylish Palmedo House looks more like a village than a single dwelling.

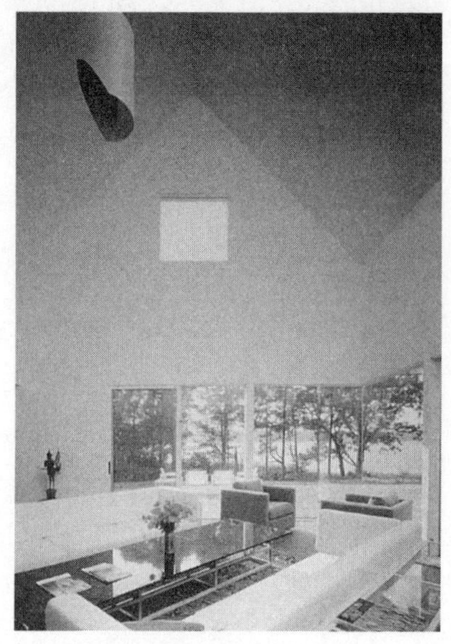

C. F. A. Voysey, and it is obvious that Greenberg has looked at Lutyens' country houses. But this is a modern house, although designed by an architect with a Classical sensibility. It admirably fulfills Palladio's call for a correspondence of the whole with the parts and the parts with the whole.

Hugh Newell Jacobsen studied at Yale under Louis Kahn, worked for Philip Johnson, and opened his own office in 1958. He established himself as a premier residential architect, winning commissions in the United States and abroad and receiving numerous design awards. Several of the awards were for restoration of historic buildings, notably the Renwick Gallery in Washington, D.C., and the Hôtel Talleyrand in Paris. A Modernist by training and inclination, Jacobsen was, nevertheless, affected by the winds of change unleashed by Venturi's little house. Starting in 1980, he evolved a hybrid style in which American regional forms and materials are combined with International Style precision, spareness, and simplicity. A house on Nantucket in shingles and white trim looks vernacular until one notices the careful proportions and refined, elegant details such as tall French doors in the living room that slide into wall pockets that also conceal shutters and screen doors. A post-and-beam Caribbean guest house with broad overhangs has the ingenuous simplicity of a beach shack. The Palladian plan and temple-like pavilions of an Ohio residence pay homage to the local Greek Revival. An Ohio country house recalls a board-and-batten Gothic Revival farmhouse. "I endeavor to design buildings that express a sense of belonging," Jacobsen says, "buildings that reflect or abstract the nearby architecture and the traditions dictated by the climate and local materials."[12]

The Palmedo House, built in 1988, reinterprets the American Colonial architecture of its location—Long Island. At first glance, the six pavilions resemble a little village, a little Amish village, judging from the austere white wood siding, the prim details, and the identical pitched roofs. Each pavilion is a perfect little "house" with identical square and vertical multi-paned windows (that open by sliding into cunning wall pockets). This sounds precious, but Jacobsen is not a romantic. The central "house" contains the living room, a three-story space open to the roof. Although the multi-paned windows are present at an upper level of the wall, the corner of the room is glazed with large, mullionless sheets of plate glass, offering dramatic views of Long Island Sound. This is an International Style device, as is the economy of detail and the clean, cool, atmosphere of the interior. On the other hand, the fireplace, which in an orthodox International Style house would be painted brick or bush-hammered concrete, is decorously built into the wall, which gives the room a traditional, civilized air. The chief idea here is to highlight the tension between old and new, between the traditional clapboarded architecture and the demands of modern life. Whereas Greenberg seamlessly resolves this tension, Jacobsen allows it to surface. If this sounds like textbook Postmodernism, it is not. Jacobsen artlessly combines new and old without the slightest hint of irony.

Jacobsen reacts to the collapse of Modernism by seeking a compromise position, while Greenberg anchors himself in the certainties of Classicism. Enrique Norten, the youngest of the three, takes a different course—he is trying to put Modernism back together again. Norten, who studied at Cornell, established his office in his native Mexico City in 1985. In a relatively short time he produced an impressive body of work that includes institutional, commercial, and residential buildings. His major projects are a services building for the media giant TELEVISA and the National School of Theater. Both incorporate bulging, metal shell-roofs that recall the 1950s buildings of the French architect-engineer Jean Prouvé. Prouvé was intent on applying new methods of construction, particularly industrialization and prefabrication. His buildings, extremely light and assembled from standardized elements, were real "machines for living." Norten, too, is preoccupied with industrial building technologies, the lighter the better. Double-tensed glass curtain walls are mysteriously supported by a steel-frame. Roofs hang by steel cables from steel masts. Slender, canted columns brace a glass-roofed portico. Railings, in a Norten design, are almost always opportunities for structural legerdemain: suspended sheets of glass, stretched steel cables, perforated metal screens.

In 1994, Norten built a house for himself and his family on a tight urban site in Mexico City. The three-story street façade is mostly a blank concrete wall; the wall facing the interior walled patio is entirely glass. The main living floor is open, except for the kitchen; the upper bedroom floor is shaded and given privacy by a redwood, louvered screen. A functionalist style pervades the house. The clinical cabinetwork is white-painted wood. A concrete wall in the dining room is bare save for the regular pattern of the formwork ties and the pour lines marks. The windows are large sections of plate glass in simple aluminum frames; a 10-foot section slides aside to entirely open the dining room to the patio. The sliding wall recalls the disappearing windows in Mies van der Rohe's Tugendhat House, but the resemblance ends here. Mies' spare interior is opulent and assertive; Norten's is austere, almost monastic: a neutral background for family life. This is an unsentimental idea of the home. Not exactly a "machine for living," but certainly machinelike in its precision and rational layout.

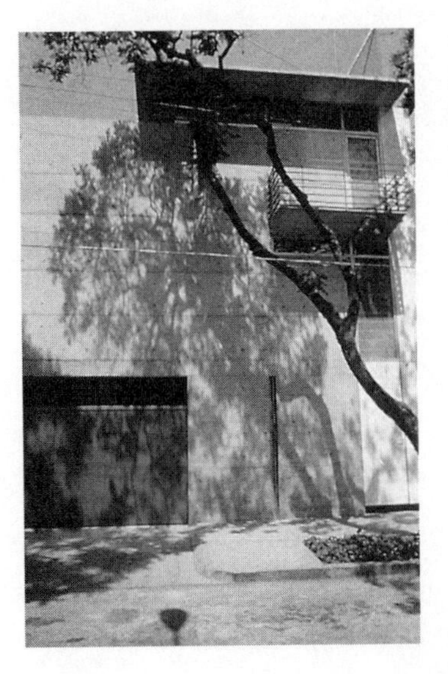

Fig. 31 (LEFT) and Fig. 32 (BELOW). Austere Modernism: House LE, designed by Enrique Norten of TEN Arquitectos.

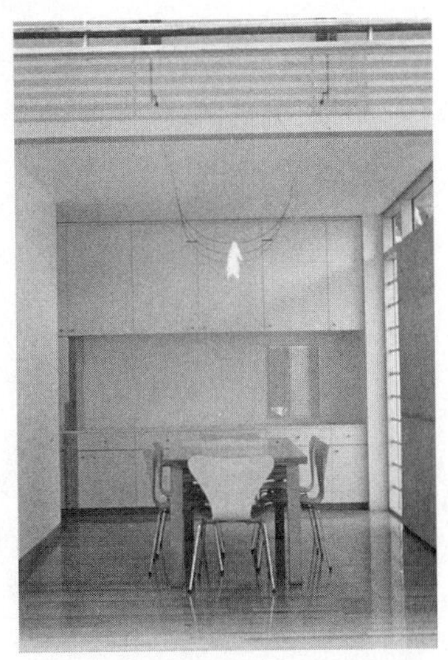

Like Greenberg and Jacobsen, Norten reflects on the past. Although his house has little to do formally with the International Style of the flat-roofed stucco villas of the 1920s—except for the white-painted circular steel columns—it shares that period's ambitions; it is highly abstract, idealistic, technophile, and lacking in applied ornament. Decoration results not from trim, but from the surface quality of the different materials—concrete, red oak flooring, etched glass—and from the relentless articulation of structural connections. Norten's buildings exhibit another feature of the International Style: they are placeless. That is, while they carefully respond to the specifics of the program and the site, they do not explicitly acknowledge their immediate regional context. Whether they are in Mexico or New Mexico—where Norten is building a heritage center—the style is the same: understated, coolly competent, cosmopolitan.

Whether one prefers the work of Greenberg, Jacobsen, or Norten is a matter of taste (I happen to like all three). The buildings are different, yet the three architects have something in common. They are serious about what they are doing, that is, their buildings exhibit a strong sense of conviction. They pay enormous attention to details. They are disciplined, but they understand their self-imposed rules well enough to occasionally break them. Moreover, while their architecture is built with a great sense of style, it is never merely stylized. That is because in their buildings, *style*—the manner of expression—is always in the service of *content*—that which is being expressed. Style without content quickly degenerates into caricature, like a speaker who makes grand gestures and rhetorical flourishes, but has nothing to say. The buildings of Greenberg, Jacobsen, and Norten, on the contrary, have a great deal to tell us about our past, our surroundings, and ourselves.

Greenberg, Jacobsen, and Norten do not describe what they do in terms of style. I think that there are a number of reasons that architects are uncomfortable talking about the subject. A suspicion of style is a heritage of the Modern Movement, which preached against the arbitrary dictates of style and fashion, while maintaining an unspoken but rigid stylistic consistency. So deep-rooted is this teaching that it remains a moral stricture on most architects, whether or not they are Modernists. Perhaps another reason for the reluctance to discuss style is fear. Fear that being linked to a particular style is to be put in a box—like most creative people, architects dislike being categorized. Also fear that talking about style will make architecture—a serious business—sound frivolous. Better to leave that to interior decorators and fashion designers, professions that architects regard with a mixture of disdain and envy. Finally, there is an unspoken fear of style because it is subject to the whims and the fancies of fashion. That fear, at least, seems to me to be ill-founded. An architecture that recognizes style—and fashion—would not be an architecture that is introspective and self-referential, as are so many contemporary buildings. It would be part of the world—not architecture for architects, but architecture for the rest of us. And that would not be a bad thing.

Coda

Richard Morris Hunt was the most celebrated American architect of the late nineteenth century. His preeminence is reflected by his appointment as the architect of two important national works: the centerpiece building of the Chicago World's Columbian Exposition, and the pedestal for the Statue of Liberty. He was feted at home and abroad. Hunt was the first architect to receive an honorary doctorate from Harvard and the first American to receive a Gold Medal from the Royal Institute of British Architects, and he was made an honorary member of the French Académie and a Chevalier of the Legion of Honor. A hundred years later, his counterpart is Frank O. Gehry. Since being awarded the prestigious Pritzker Prize in 1989, Gehry has gone on to win more honors than any other living architect, including such major arts awards as the Dorothy and Lillian Gish

Prize (a non-architectural award of which he is the first recipient) and the Japanese Praemium Imperiale, the Nobel of the art world. Even the staid American Institute of Architects, which had previously shunned Gehry in lieu of more mainstream practitioners, awarded him its top accolade, the AIA Gold Medal.

No pair of architects could be more dissimilar than this distinctly odd couple, the proper High Society favorite of the Gilded Age and the untidy bohemian from Santa Monica. Yet they bear comparison. They were both late bloomers. Gehry was 48 when he gained national recognition. Until then, he had been running his own office in Los Angeles for almost twenty years, building shopping centers, suburban offices, department stores, and apartments in competent but unremarkable renditions of L.A. modern. The project that brought him to national attention was his own remodeled house: a nondescript bungalow encased in an unsettling Cubist composition of unpainted plywood, corrugated metal, and chain-link fencing. The odd shapes and unorthodox materials marked Gehry as a maverick. That was in 1978. Unexpectedly, he attracted a broad range of commissions, not only residential clients, but also museums, public institutions, universities, corporations, and developers, and not only in the United States but around the world.

Hunt was 43 when he came into his own. He had established an architectural practice in New York in 1855, almost immediately on his return from the Ecole des Beaux-Arts. He was moderately successful, achieving local renown for the Tribune Building, an early New York skyscraper. Despite his Parisian background, Hunt worked in the prevalent Ruskinian Gothic style. Of his Presbyterian Hospital in downtown Manhattan, the architectural critic Montgomery Schuyler wrote: "The building is of Gothic design with very red brick, and very irregular stone dressings, which, it must be confessed regretfully, are not pleasing to the eye."[3] For his next project, the Lenox Library, Hunt tried something different. He borrowed from the French Neo-Grec style, popularized by Labrouste in the Bibliothèque Sainte Geneviève, adding Renaissance details and his own characteristically vigorous surface modeling. The result was a startling departure from convention, a monochrome limestone block of imposing dignity. The Lenox Library (which stood on Fifth Avenue on the site of the present-day Frick Collection) marked a shift in architectural taste, away from Ruskin to a grand and frankly aesthetic Classicism. The 1880s was a decade of great prosperity, and newly wealthy New Yorkers eagerly sought out Hunt's architectural blend of good taste and ostentatious display. He obliged them in a string of high-profile commissions: magnificent mansions along Fifth Avenue, country houses on Long Island, and palatial "cottages" in Newport, Rhode Island. Hunt died in 1895, but in the last seven years of his life, he completed more than fifty projects.

Biltmore House in Asheville, North Carolina, is a good example of his stylistic prowess. Hunt modeled the design of this 250-room residence on the Château de Blois, whose style is not the severe Classicism of the Italian Renaissance favored by architects such as Charles McKim, but the more ornate and picturesque French Renaissance. To a modern visitor, the spires, turrets, and steep slate roofs of Biltmore recall Disneyland's Sleeping Beauty Castle, which is not surprising since Disney also used a Loire Valley chateau—the Château d'Ussé—as his model. But the comparison does Hunt an injustice, for his design is neither prettified nor quaint. His client, George W. Vanderbilt, was a young bachelor (he married soon after the house was finished), and for him Hunt created an architecture that is robust, masculine, and immensely self-assured, not in the least like a fairytale.

Vanderbilt was drawn to French chateaux, which Hunt showed him during a whirlwind European tour, since young George and his wealthy family imagined themselves American aristocrats. There are coats of arms bearing Vs all over the house. Hunt provides his client with an imagined

Fig. 33. Richard Morris Hunt's Biltmore House in Asheville, North Carolina, 1892-1895.

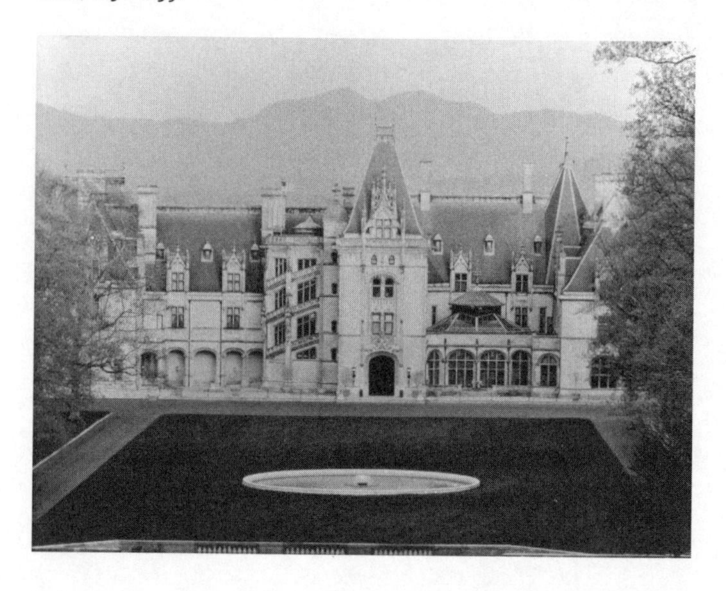

regal setting, but deals with the past in his own peculiar way. Although he modeled the building on Blois, he makes no attempt to create a replica of the sixteenth-century chateau, but draws details from other buildings of the period and recombines them into an original whole. Nor does he try to create the illusion that this is a sixteenth-century building—there is no artificial weathering, no aging effect no simulated historicism. The interior is modern, bright, and open. The focus of the main floor is a glass-roofed conservatory, a common nineteenth-century feature. The stonework of the house is impeccable, much crisper and more sharply defined than at Blois. Hunt was no antiquarian, and modern American technology abounds. The floors of fireproof hollow tile are supported by steel I-beams and the steep slate roofs by steel roof trusses. Cast iron replaces wrought iron and high-quality bricks, fired in the estate brickworks, back-up the limestone walls. Equally novel are the elevators and telephones, electrical lighting, hot and cold running water, and forced air central heating. There is no doubt that for Hunt, Biltmore is an up-to-the-minute *modern* building. That is part of its style, too.

Like Hunt, Frank Gehry enlists novel materials in his buildings. The Guggenheim Museum in Bilbao, Spain, for example, is clad in titanium, previously used chiefly for building aircraft. The metallic walls curve, twist, and turn.

Fig. 34. The Guggenheim Museum in Bilbao, Spain, designed by Frank O. Gehry, 1991-1997.

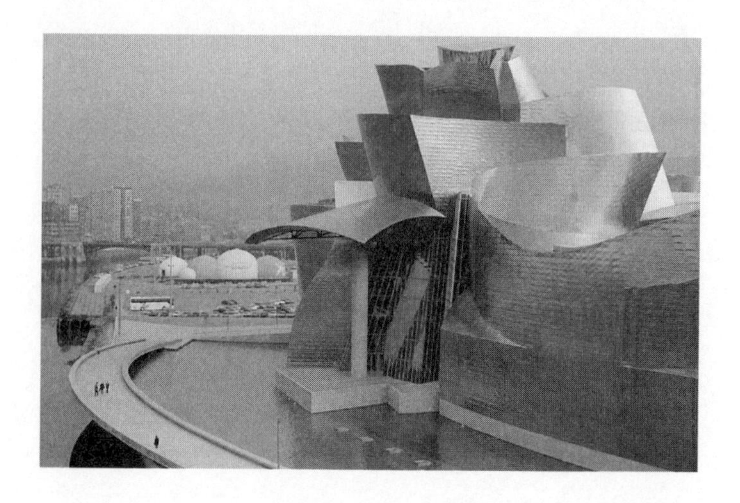

One part of the building slides under an adjoining bridge; another emerges from a reflecting pool. Bilbainos refer to the museum as the "artichoke," which comes close to describing it, if you can imagine a gleaming, metallic artichoke more than two hundred feet high. The seeming disorder—a chaotic collision of forms—has no architectural precedent. This is not sculptural architecture, it is walk-in sculpture.

"The plan is the generator" preached Le Corbusier, but with Gehry, the plan is the result. He appears to design from the outside in. The building as a composition comes first, the interior spaces follow. This implies that he shoehorns functions into the building, which is not the case. The Guggenheim has three distinct types of gallery spaces: traditional, skylit rooms for displaying its permanent collection of early Modernist art; a long boat-like space for temporary installations; and 11 smaller galleries, each with its own character, each dedicated to the works of a selected living artist. The artichoke accommodates them all. The building may appear offhanded, but there is nothing haphazard about the way it is organized.

Gehry's talent is his exceptional formal imagination; his skill as an architect is to reconcile the forms he imagines with the functional demands of his client. And, of course, to find ways to build those forms. This is generally done without fuss. The titanium sheets simply follow the churning surfaces like shingles on a Shingle Style roof; limestone is used in a similarly unaffected fashion, without articulated joints. Gehry shares a minimalist approach to details with the early architects of the International Style, but he deploys these details to different ends. By removing familiar elements such as coping strips, fascias, and trim, he accentuates the sculptural quality of his buildings. There are no roofs or walls or windows in the Guggenheim, there are only swirling and twisting planes of metal, stone, and glass. An architecture critic once described Gehry as "a smart man from Hollywood," which nicely captures the architect's blend of exuberant showmanship and canny behind-the-scenes savvy.

Although sophisticated building techniques and innovative materials play a major role in Gehry's buildings, like Hunt, he keeps technology off center stage. In that regard, he repudiates the mannered industrial style that pervades the work of many contemporary architects. Neither is he nostalgic about the past. Gehry rejects both the moralistic functionalism of the International Style and the traditions of Classicism. Architects have broken rules in the past, but rarely this unequivocally and totally.

Gehry, like Hunt, has changed the course of architecture. That is, he has made us look at our surroundings in a different way. The world of Gehry's buildings is, at first glance, an odd place. The line between order and disorder is a thin one, and it is difficult to know what is intended and what is accidental. But his colliding forms and agitated architecture are curiously unthreatening. This is the way we live today, Gehry seems to be saying, why not enjoy it?

Notes

DRESSING UP

1 For an excellent discussion of the constructed reality versus the image of modern buildings, see Edward R. Ford, *The Details of Modern Architecture* (Cambridge, Mass.: MIT Press, 1990) and *The Details of Modern Architecture, vol. 2: 1928 to 1998* (Cambridge, Mass.: MIT Press, 1996).

2 Vincent Scully, *Architecture: The Natural and the Man-made* (New York: St. Martin's Press, 1991), 55-56.

3 George Hersey, *The Lost Meaning of Classical Architecture: Speculations on Ornament from Vitruvius to Venturi* (Cambridge, Mass.: MIT Press, 1988), 23.

4 John Summerson, *The Classical Language of Architecture* (London: Thames & Hudson, 1980), 15.

5 Heinrich Klotz, *The History of Postmodern Architecture,*

trans. Radka Donnell (Cambridge, Mass.: MIT Press, 1988), 179.

6 Anne Hollander, *Sex and Suits* (New York: Knopf, 1994), 141.

IN AND OUT OF FASHION

1 See John Tauranac, *The Empire State Building: The Making of a Landmark* (New York: Scribner, 1995), 184-97.

2 Fernand Braudel, *Capitalism and Material Life 1400-1800*, trans. Miriam Kochan (New York: Harper Colophon, 1975), 239.

3 John W. Cook and Heinrich Klotz, *Conversations with Architects* (London: Lund Humphries, 1973), 94.

4 Raymond Hood, "Exterior Architecture of Office Buildings," *Architectural Forum*, vol. 41, no. 3 (September 1924), 97-98.

5 John Summerson, *Heavenly Mansions: And Other Essays on Architecture* (New York: Norton, 1963), 12-13.

6 *The Architecture of Frank Gehry* (New York: Rizzoli, 1986), 161.

7 Ibid., 236.

STYLE

1 Marcus Binney, "Books, yes," *The Times* (March 11, 1996).

2 Jonathan Glancey, "Cross-Channel sibling has kept to the storyline," *Independent* (December 17, 1996).

3 Ralph Adams Cram, "Style in American Architecture," *Architectural Record* (September 1913), 237.

4 Ibid.

5 Roger Scruton, *The Aesthetics of Architecture* (Princeton, N.J.: Princeton University Press, 1979), 16.

6 Peter Collins, *Changing Ideals in Modern Architecture 1750-1950* (Montreal: McGill University Press, 1965), 65.

7 Jacques François Blondel, *Cours d'Architecture*, vol. 1 (Paris: Desaint, 1771), 401.

8 Andrea Palladio, *The Four Books of Architecture*, trans. Isaac Ware (New York: Dover Publications, 1965), 1.

9 Scruton, *The Aesthetics of Architecture*, 262.

10 Robert Venturi, "Mother's House 25 Years Later," in *Mother's House: The Evolution of Vanna Venturi's House in Chestnut Hill*, ed. Frederic Schwartz (New York: Rizzoli, 1992), 37.

11 Allan Greenberg, "What is Modern Architecture," in *Allan Greenberg*, Architectural Monographs No. 39 (London: Academy Editions, 1995), 11.

12 "The AD 100 Architects," *Architectural Digest*, vol. 48, no. 9 (1991), 124.

13 Quoted in Robert A. M. Stern, Thomas Mellins, and

David Fishman, *New York 1900: Architecture and Urbanism in the Gilded Age* (New York: Monacelli Press, 1999), 260.

Index